FAITH ON THE MARCH

FAITH
ON THE
MARCH

BY

A. H. Macmillan

PRENTICE-HALL, INC.

ENGLEWOOD CLIFFS, N.J.

Printed in the United States of America

30141

CONTENTS

Part Three: THE NEW WORLD SURVIVES

INTRODUCTION

To the reader:

A. H. Macmillan is known to Jehovah's witnesses all over the world. His long and prominent association with the Watch Tower Bible and Tract Society and his faithful record of service as a Christian minister have endeared him to his many friends.

Toward the end of 1955 Mr. Macmillan asked permission to use the Society's files to write an account of his experiences in the ministry. Since he is a trusted member of the headquarters staff, he was granted permission. A few months ago he informed me the work was finished, and at his request I agreed to read the manuscript for technical accuracy. I soon found myself engrossed in the story which the account of his life and association with Jehovah's witnesses had produced.

This book is more than the story of one man's growing faith. I believe Mr. Macmillan has made a sincere effort to capture and portray the very essence of the religion that he acknowledges has given meaning to his life. He reveals Jehovah's witnesses as human. He admits their mistakes and explains why no human organization can be infallible. At the same time he reveals their hopes, and presents sound Scriptural reasons for the appeal of these hopes to all kinds of men.

The book is a straightforward and truthful account. It is unique only in the personal experiences of A. H. Macmillan. In many other respects it could be the story of any one of hundreds of Jehovah's witnesses whom I have known.

N. H. KNORR,
President, Watch Tower Bible
and Tract Society of Pennsylvania

Brooklyn, New York

PART ONE

"CALLED
OUT OF
DARKNESS"

1

A TURNING-POINT

I AM A WHITE-HAIRED OLD MAN, in my eightieth year of life, as I begin to tell you these facts.

For nigh onto sixty years I have been associated with a movement that today is commanding world attention on a widening scale. It is a religious movement that has seemed new and recent to millions of people, a movement that has been fought tooth, tongue and pen by the dominant religions of this world, a movement that has been misrepresented, persecuted, cursed and damned, prayed against to the God of heaven, and subjected to mobbing, bans, confiscation and proscriptions, driven underground by Nazi, Fascist and Communist dictators, all this under the influence of religious leaders, all of them together up in arms against this lone movement.

I know. I have gone through enough of it along with this movement to know whereof I speak and write.

I myself have spent nine long months in prison for my faith before I was released with my fellow-sufferers and then

3

cleared of all the untrue charges that put us behind bars. Since then I have talked to hundreds of young men likewise put behind bars for their faith.

In the course of the years I have traveled through many countries, including Palestine where Jesus and the apostles preached the same message; talked to hundreds of thousands of people from the public platform, frequently through the aid of an interpreter, yes, and from house to house as the apostles did; and at present it is my privilege to address untold numbers by the modern means of radio over a pioneer station in New York City, answering people's questions, giving them Bible counsel delivered straight from the shoulder.

From the horse-and-buggy days, when as a young lad I learned to handle an ox-cart, I have lived down through the years into this age of jet-propulsion and thermonuclear explosives, through two world wars into the most terrifying situation of all human history. But I'm not afraid, for being with this religious movement has made me fearless of the future. I'm not afraid of what is ahead of the human race in the purposes of the great Creator, even though come, as it must, the worst time of trouble that mankind has ever experienced.

To know a movement you've got to live with it, even be an official in it, as I have been. Besides that, I have lived through to the end of two presidencies of the religious society that governs this movement, and I'm now living under the presidency of the third man in that office in the Society. I've seen things grow, I've seen the understanding of things clear up, I've gone through the ups and downs of this religious movement. Yet I am holding on, and that with more zest than ever before. More than ever I am convinced that it is right, that it has the truth, that it is giving a right lead to all the people of good will throughout the earth. Why?

I FOUND A FAITH

Have you ever wondered whether you had the right religion and have you tried to find the right one, to find the truth that solved your questions about God and his purposes toward mankind? I have, and I know what a battle it means. But it's worth the battle. Today people are feeling after religion, because life without the truth about God and man does not satisfy. These people fumbling about don't know where this world is going. Once I, too, did not know. I did not know where I myself was going.

As a lad in my teens, I was just an ordinary boy, with a desire for play and fun that all of us enjoy. Still I had a deep feeling that I would like to know more about God and why this earth was made and people put on it for such a short time, only to die and go no one knows where, perhaps never to see family or friends again.

Asking questions on the subject from those who were supposed to know the answers, I received little or no information. But I kept on looking, believing that the answers must be somewhere to be found. They are, for I have found what I was looking for. I was still a young man. But that makes no difference. What I have found thousands of people are still finding every year. And they are people just like you and me, because they come from all nationalities, races, walks of life and are of all ages. Truth is no respecter of persons. It attracts all kinds of persons and those who are following it find themselves being drawn ever closer together, away from a world that is showing a rapidly diminishing regard for personal, or even national, integrity.

Now I do know where I am going. I am confident too that I know where the world is going. I have been watching it travel that road for almost sixty years. A short space in the span of history, you say? Perhaps, but these years are destiny-shaping, never to be repeated. These are years that were longed for centuries ago, years that were seen in prophetic vision, years that are climaxing six thousand years of human history. Why am I so sure of that? Because that is the message I have learned from the Bible and I have seen it being fulfilled with my own eyes during the eighty years of my life.

From my first glimpse of the promises held out to sick and dying mankind my hope in what that message of the Bible has revealed has not faded. Right there I determined to find out more about what the Bible teaches so that I might be able to help others like myself who are seeking knowledge about the Almighty God, Jehovah, and his good purposes toward mankind.

THE FAITH OF MY FATHER TESTED

My first real opportunity came sooner than I had anticipated. After about a year of study I was called home to see my father, who was dangerously ill. Like many people he had always been a strong believer in his religion. I wondered how he would react to my presentation of what I had learned since I last saw him. It was so different from what he had taught me. Being still a youth, I journeyed home to Canada with some misgivings as to my ability to inform my father, for he was a well-educated man. However, I determined to discuss my new-found beliefs with him if at all possible, trusting the Lord to help me show him the things I had learned about Jehovah's purpose to bless mankind.

After arriving home, I went to my father's bedside. I saw he was very weak and would not live much longer. He was an old man, about the age I am now. As I approached the bed, he held out his hand and, with a faint smile, he said: "Son, I'm glad you came home to see me before I pass away. You were the only one of my children that gave much evidence of deep interest in religion, and I want to talk to you about the Bible.

"I believe many more people will be saved than my minister has led me to believe," he continued.

This surprised me somewhat because my father was a Calvinist and believed in predestination. However, I was pleased that he should feel that way and replied, "I agree with you, Father. I'm sure the Bible shows God is willing that all men should be saved, and come to a knowledge of the truth, and if any are lost, it is because they refuse to take the way he has opened up. God did not predestinate that any individuals should be lost and tormented forever, as many believe."

As we went on with our talks I could see father seemed no longer interested in what Calvin taught. Apparently he had been reading and thinking very seriously about the Bible itself. He started asking me questions about the new world mentioned in the Bible. Surprised again, I asked what led him to that line of thinking and he replied: "Before I became so ill I read a book issued by one of the Bible and tract societies in the United States, and that answered many questions that have bothered me." Then he told me the title of the book. You can imagine my surprise and delight to find it was the same book I was studying and from which I had already received so much comfort and satisfying knowledge.

This lively hope being kindled in my father seemed to rally him somewhat and for the next few weeks we had many happy studies together. He would ask the neighbors, who came to visit him, to join us in our studies, and those did. The new world was generally our theme. I pointed out from the Bible that the earth was created to be inhabited by perfect men and women who would live forever in peace without anything to mar their complete happiness. None of them had ever heard of such a possibility. But it sounded good to them.

HOPE OF A NEW LIFE

All who joined us in our studies said they believed the Bible was the Word of God, and they would accept what was written there. Some of them had read only a little in the Bible, and they soon learned that it contained many things they had never realized. We read that the earth would become as beautiful as the garden of Eden was when Adam and Eve were living in it as their God-given estate. I was able to find for them where that was written in the Bible.

Naturally, what the condition of our health would be at that time came up for discussion. I assured them, one of the prophets had said that in that new system of things to be established after Armageddon no one would say he was sick. Furthermore, it had been revealed to the apostle John that there would be no more crying or pain—not even any more death! My father, who was suffering much physical pain, said: "How I wish that time were here now!" And all agreed with him, for they were thinking of their own loved ones, many of whom were no longer with them. Then I read an excerpt from our Bible-study aid that brought tears of joy to my father's eyes: [1]

> The human race are God's children by creation—the work of his hands—and his purpose with reference to them is clearly revealed in his Word. Our Lord, and all the prophets since the world began, declare that the human race is to be restored to that glorious perfection Adam had.
>
> This is the portion God has arranged to give to the human race. And what a glorious portion! Forget for a moment the misery and woe, degradation and sorrow that still prevail on account of sin, and picture before your mental vision the glory of the perfect earth. . . . There sickness shall be no more; not an ache nor a pain—not even the fear of such things. Think of all the pictures of comparative health and beauty of human form and feature that you have ever seen,

and know that perfect humanity will be of still surpassing loveliness. The inward purity and mental and moral perfection will stamp and glorify every radiant countenance. Such will earth's society be; and weeping bereaved ones will have their tears wiped away, when Christ's kingdom work is completed.

HOPE FOR THE DEAD

Of course this brought up a number of questions, some of which may be in your own mind. One was, what hope can we have in that new world if we die before that happy time arrives? This I could answer through the clear-cut promise of the resurrection. Then my father asked me the direct question: "Son, will I be lonesome in the grave while I am waiting for the kingdom to begin its work of filling the earth with perfection?"

That was a question a young man could not readily answer to the satisfaction of an older person who had never thought along that line.

In reply I asked him: "Father, did you sleep well last night?"

He answered, "Yes, my son, I did after the doctor gave me some sleeping pills."

"Were you lonesome while you were asleep?"

"No, I was not. I wish I could sleep all the time, for then I feel no pain."

Then I remembered something I had read about Job, who was suffering much bodily pain after he lost everything he had including his family. I read to my father what Job had said: [2]

"Oh that thou wouldest hide me in Sheol [the grave], . . . until thy wrath be past, . . . Thou wouldest call, and I would answer thee." . . . "There the wicked cease from troubling;

And there the weary are at rest. There the prisoners are at ease together; They hear not the voice of the taskmaster. The small and the great are there: And the servant is free from his master."

"So you see, father," I explained, "the dead are in a death sleep and know nothing while in that condition, so how could they be lonesome? Too, the Bible says 'the dead know not anything.' When you fall asleep in death no one will bother you; you will have no pain either. When God's proper time comes and Jesus calls you, then you will come to life in a world where there will be no pain, sorrow or death."

As my father breathed his last I read to him the heart-cheering words of the twenty-first chapter of Revelation: "Behold, the tabernacle of God is with men, and he will dwell with them, and they shall be his people, and God himself shall be with them, and be their God. And God shall wipe away all tears from their eyes; and there shall be no more death, neither sorrow, nor crying, neither shall there be any more pain: for the former things are passed away." Yes, my father died with a glorious hope and I know the sting of death was relieved by that hope.

That same hope, as outlined in God's Word, has been mine for over half a century. It has brought me peace of mind and joy of heart. It has sustained me through many dark hours. It has taught me a reverential fear of my God and a deep and sincere love for my fellow man. It has brought to me a new way of life.

CIVILIZATION'S SHAKY FOUNDATION

I do not need to tell you that mankind are enjoying many comforts and pleasures in this life, yet still there is great fear as to what the future holds for this generation. You know the nations are armed to the teeth with the most deadly weapons

ever invented or constructed. Those who should know tell us
bombs are now made that could destroy a good-sized city in a
few moments. They also tell us that deadly guided missiles
carrying atomic warheads can be accurately delivered to dis-
tant targets in a matter of minutes. They further claim that
other death-dealing weapons exist that are too terrible to talk
about. Even limited tests are restricted for fear of the results.

Some believe that the Communists are determined to destroy
every nation on earth that will not come around to their
terms or surrender to their way of life, which is slavery for
the many, and all the luxuries of the land for a few ruthless
rulers or dictators. The "free nations," at the risk of bank-
rupting their own economy, are spending billions of dollars
to aid others remain "free." But even if compromises are
achieved, even if the policy of co-existence is developed to
where it seems workable, is there not only one inevitable outcome?

On what kind of foundation do you think modern security
rests? Can you truly be happy at prospects of our future,
with the nations sitting on stockpiles of thermonuclear explosives? With fear, hatred and suspicion sitting at the conference table, with distrust and deceit undermining even hard-
won peace negotiations and efforts at disarmament, how small
a spark would be needed to set the world aflame? Is the destiny of modern civilization dependent solely on the volatile
emotions of selfish, greedy and unscrupulous dictators who
loudly hold forth the palm of peace while only partially con-
cealing the strong arm of fission-fusion might?

What is your honest opinion of world conditions? Beware
of shrugging it off with a noncommittal air of, "Oh well, we
have survived in the past, we'll find a way out." Is there any
evidence whatsoever that the direction of the world has radi-
cally changed in the relation of man to man, nation to nation?
Does the history of the world—even of the last few decades—

reveal we have found a safer, saner approach to solving international controversies?

How far must we go before we have reached "the end"?

Those who turn to the Bible learn that everything we now
experience was foretold by the prophets of old, who spoke
under divine inspiration. Why do the clergymen of Christendom remain silent? Why do they say nothing about the
threatened end of this system of things or about the blessings
of the new world, which are certain to follow the battle of
the great day of God Almighty so near at hand? It is only by
such a war as Armageddon, fought by Jehovah God and his
invisible forces, that the earth can be cleansed of all unright-
eousness and the way opened for lasting peace on earth. Consider the evidences for yourself. The Bible was written by
men like us, men from all walks of life, but men whose faith
surpassed all fear of man. You can read the Bible and understand it, too.

WHY MY FAITH ABIDES

When I first began to look for these answers they were not
nearly so apparent as they now are. In fact, the evidences we
now accept as everyday occurrences did not even exist. They
were at that time only prophecies of the Bible that were being
interpreted in many different ways by different groups. But
one group of earnest Bible students presented matters in a
way that made sense to me. Now I see my confidence was
well grounded.

You ask me why I am still an active part of that movement,
why my zeal is keener and my conviction stronger than ever?
I'll tell you. It's because I've lived to realize already much of
the hope that so filled my young life. It's because I've lived to
see prophecies of the Bible which we held dear and sacred—
yet which were mocked and scorned by unbelievers—already

come true. It's because I've lived to see this same movement hunted and persecuted by those who claimed to serve God until it lay beaten in death—only to survive and come to re-birth in a new way of life, reorganized for an even more powerful work, yet dedicated to the same standards of right-eousness which have characterized its operation from the be-ginning. I have seen this movement hold fast to those stand-ards, refusing to compromise them for the sake of expediency. I have seen ambitious men rise up within the organization and seek to pervert it, only to meet with complete defeat because the majority of those associated with this movement are un-alterably dedicated to serve God, not man. I have found com-panionship, yes, real brotherhood, with people of all races and nations. These are the things I have desired from my youth.

Can you tell me why a man who—not once, but many times—has seen things come into existence that he was told he would see; why a man who has watched the outworking of God's foretold purpose and the fulfillment of prophecies;—can you, I ask, tell me why such a man should *not* have faith? My faith is stronger each day. And having seen so much come true already I am more and more confident that those things for which I still hope will some day be realized as well.

FACING THE FUTURE WITHOUT FEAR

I am most thankful to share with you this message of hope that is now being preached in many lands throughout the earth. Because they see that this old system of things is doomed, hundreds of thousands of people are grasping and devouring the knowledge now available on the subject. This hope is tangible, reasonable and real. Men and women on this earth, even with many troubles, do not want to grow old and die. No, they want to stay right here. Don't you? Well, that is not surprising, for man was created to live on this earth and he enjoys himself when he has a reasonable amount of the blessings now possible to obtain.

To every thoughtful person it is apparent that mankind has reached a turning-point in history. A day of judgment is upon us. Even Satan the Devil himself knows that but a short time remains in which the human race, yes, this generation, must decide the greatest issue ever put before mankind. The issue is this: Will you continue to support and bear up a system of things that has filled the earth with suffering, sorrow, sin and death? Or will you choose, and fit yourself for God's love-filled new world?

Running with the world means, in the near future, eternal death. Walking with God and the New World society and devoting yourself to the principles of the new world will mean peace, happiness and real freedom with an endless life in perfection on a paradise earth.

Everywhere people are rallying to this hope. My personal experience may help you.

With you I hope I can live through the fast-approaching world catastrophe, the most appalling in all universal history, and then enter alive into the new world that Almighty God in his love has promised to establish for all those who seek to know him and to love and serve him. So now let me get along with my story, setting out the facts and experiences of my personal history that have some importance, some bearing on the big, decisive issues that face you and me.

2

BEGINNING A NEW WAY

WHEN YOU CHANGE OVER the pattern of your thinking it means changing your way of life, yet the apostle Paul said that for Christians it is necessary to: [1] "Quit being fashioned after this system of things, but be transformed by making your mind over, that you may prove to yourselves the good and acceptable and complete will of God." That is the battle that goes with finding the right religion.

It was this interest in solving the questions about God, interest in him as a personality who loves, thinks—even hates—that led to the understanding of God's will now being proclaimed world-wide by Jehovah's witnesses. Religions for centuries had been placing emphasis on man and his salvation or damnation, with little regard to the name of the God responsible for these destinies. All concepts of God were fashioned, not particularly from the Bible, but from man's interest in himself.

For centuries men had depended on the religious clergy to attend to the matter of salvation. If the layman concerned himself with the Bible, it was viewed almost as heresy; he was a doubter. This made salvation dependent upon men.

Eventually some rebelled. They wanted to show that men had nothing to do with the salvation of others. So they said Almighty God had fixed their destinies before he ever created one of the human family. Each man was predestined before birth to a heaven of bliss or a hell of fiery torment.

Another reformer said, "This conception of God is my conception of the Devil. If a man is not saved it's his own fault, because God has made all arrangements for him to obtain salvation, but mankind will not accept it." This puts God in competition with the Devil and robs God of his power because it looks like the Devil is getting more converts.

If we are to obtain the Scriptural perspective of God's way of salvation, then we must realize that a period of readjustment is necessary. Throughout this time of revaluation we will be faced with many mental and spiritual pitfalls. Some may seem small and insignificant, but to survive them we must completely subordinate our personal preferences. To rely on Jehovah's direction is the way of wisdom.[2]

SEEKING GOD'S WILL

Sometimes small happenings can affect one's entire life for good or for bad and can extend even into the lives of others to change their course. Some have said that just such a chain of reactions was set in motion when, about 1870, a young man (whose life, later, had considerable influence on my own), upon hearing religious singing in a little dingy hall on one of the dark streets of Allegheny, Pennsylvania, turned aside and walked in.

While in many respects this young man was quite like most boys of his age, in other ways he was unusual indeed. Born of Scottish-Irish parents February 16, 1852, he had been brought up in the Calvinistic doctrine to believe that men before birth were selected or predestinated by God to spend eternity either in the joys of heaven or in the torments of hell. This did not seem reasonable to his inquiring mind; so at an early age he had begun searching for the truth.

From earliest youth he had been extremely devoted to the service of God. In fact, his mother had dedicated him to the work of the Lord when he was born. So he was a serious-minded young man; he wanted to serve Jehovah God to the best of his ability. But when still a lad he had become so concerned about the doctrine of immortality of the soul and eternal torment that he could not rest. He was completely unsettled in mind.

"That's not reasonable," he would insist; "that's not God-like. It just can't be true."

However, with nothing else to take its place, at the age of fourteen he would go out Saturday nights to where men gathered on Sundays to loaf, and would write Bible texts on the sidewalk with colored chalk. In this way he had hoped to attract their attention, so that they might accept Christ and avoid being lost and going to eternal torment.

At this early age his boundless energy was demonstrated in his eagerness to advertise God's will for man as he saw it. All the time he wanted to be doing something. Finally he left the Presbyterian Church because its teaching on doctrine was too narrow; he joined the Congregational Church, which he found more liberal. He had become particularly interested in the Y.M.C.A. "There's the place I can work with other young men," he reasoned. He had never wanted to sit around the church looking pious or just listening to singing and someone preaching on matters that were unreasonable, horrifying and unlike a God of love. He wanted to be active—trying to save men from going to eternal damnation. So he had worked and studied, continuing to search for the truth.

TRADITIONALISM ENCOURAGES INFIDELITY

He had examined all the different creeds—read up on what they generally taught. He had found disappointment in all of them. All this while he was trying to find something that would blend the obvious attributes of the Most High God, his love, justice, wisdom and power. He reasoned simply that if a theory or a doctrine does not square with those four attributes it must be wrong and any approach to Bible study must keep those four basic principles in mind. Any doctrine that violates any one of the attributes of God or which raises contradictions among them could not originate with God because he does not deny himself.

In discouragement he finally turned to an investigation of the claims of the leading Oriental religions, all of which he found to be unworthy of credence; hence we see him arriving at manhood's estate with a mind unsatisfied, a mind which, despite all efforts to the contrary, was still subject to its occasional bad hours on account of its "first impression" on the eternal torment theory.

"What is left to believe?" he finally asked himself. "If all the different religions that I have investigated can't present a clear and understandable picture of the Bible, then the Bible itself must be unreliable, so why believe it?" Like many serious thinkers before and since, finding the traditional teachings of religious Christendom untenable, he was falling an easy prey to the logic of infidelity.

At the age of seventeen, then, this had become his conclusion: "Now my father is in business here in Pittsburgh and is doing quite well. There is no use in my trying to find out anything reasonable about the future from any of the creeds or even from the Bible, so I'm just going to forget the whole thing and give all my attention to business. If I make some money I can use that to help suffering humanity, even though I cannot do them any good spiritually."

With that in mind he had thrown all of his dynamic force and personality into his father's business and it had really begun to prosper. He and his father had developed the idea of a chain of stores in several communities and soon had expanded their one store in Allegheny into additional establishments there and in adjacent cities. Seemingly he was well on the way to realizing his ambition to organize a corporation that would operate all over the United States. It was while he was in this frame of mind that something happened—the chance encounter that seemed to alter the pattern of his entire life.

THE BIBLE STRENGTHENS WAVERING FAITH

On this evening about 1870 he had been walking along one of the dark streets in Allegheny when he heard singing. He paused for a moment. Being young, he had an insatiable thirst for knowledge. As a reverential lad, he still had a desire for faith in the Supreme Being. He had heard that religious services were conducted here, so he asked himself, "Is it possible that the handful of people who meet here have something more sensible to offer than the creeds of the great churches?" He turned, entered the dusty little mission, and sat down to listen to the sermon.

The preacher was Jonas Wendell. His exposition of the Scriptures was not too clear; many questions were left unanswered. But one thing was certain: this youth's wavering faith in the inspiration of the Bible was immeasurably strengthened; he was now convinced from what he had heard that the records of the apostles and prophets are indissolubly linked. Here was something upbuilding, something sensible to a sensitive and inquiring young mind.

A renewed determination to continue his search for the truth opened a new chapter in this young man's life. Taking down his already well-worn Bible, he began a careful and systematic study of the Bible itself. As he read he thought, and the more he pondered the more convinced he became that the time was drawing near for the wise watching ones of the Lord's children to get a clear picture of God's purposes.

Fired now with real enthusiasm, he approached several young men with whom he had been associating, some in a business way and others socially. He told them of his rekindled interest, of his purpose to continue his direct study of the Bible without any consideration of established creeds. Immediately recognizing the possibilities, they said, "Well, suppose we get together and study in a systematic way during certain hours each week."

So it started. This young man, who at eighteen years of age organized this little Bible class, was to become one of the best-known Bible students of his generation. He was to become one of the best-loved and the most hated—one of the most praised and most maligned men in modern religious history.

That was Charles Taze Russell, later globally known as Pastor Russell.

JESUS' RANSOM REVEALS GOD'S ATTRIBUTES

The study method these young men adopted was simple but effective and has set the pattern for Bible study of Jehovah's witnesses ever since. It was based on the method used by the Christians of the first century.[3] Someone would raise a question. They would discuss it. They would look up all related scriptures on the point and then, when they were satisfied on the harmony of these texts, they would finally state their conclusion and make a record of it.

Their findings did not come all at once. They soon learned that the Bible clearly taught that the soul is not immortal and that when a person dies he is actually dead, unconscious, and that the wages of sin is death.[4] This was certainly a departure from the spiritual fare they had been receiving through the creeds based on tradition. It enabled them to discern answers to questions they never could have understood otherwise.

They learned that God had not created man to die. The father of the human race, Adam, had been created perfect and had been given a perfect wife; had been placed in a perfect home under perfect conditions and had been advised that obedience to the divine law would enable him to maintain this way of life in perfection.[5] The Scriptures revealed to them that Adam violated the law of God and was sentenced to death and was driven out of his perfect home to eke out a bare existence in the unfinished earth until death overtook him.[6] While he was undergoing this sentence Adam, for the first time, exercised his power and authority to reproduce; [7] and under the law of heredity his children were born under the condemnation of death and without the right to life.[8] Being unconscious in death, they were without hope unless some provision should be made to restore them to life.[9]

Although this early period of study revealed only the general outlines of God's purposes, it was a profitable time of unlearning many long-cherished errors as well. For instance, in considering man's hope of restoration to life they asked themselves, What did Adam really lose? Did he lose a chance to go to heaven?—as they all had been taught to believe. No, they discovered. After careful study of the inspired Record they summed up Adam's loss in these three things: First, he lost fellowship with God; second, his beautiful home in Eden —he was forced out; third, he lost life and his right to it, for he was told that he would have to struggle in the sweat of his face until he returned to the ground from which he was taken. That means that he would die in the effort to keep alive. This added new meaning to Jesus' words,[10] "For the Son of man is come to seek and to save that which was lost." Now how was this to be accomplished? They began to see that for Jesus to qualify as a redeemer he must at some time and under some condition have an opportunity to buy back these three things that were lost to the human race through Adam.

Now, for the first time, they could see God's attributes in true perspective! His justice required Adam's execution for disobedience, yet his love was revealed in promising a ransom for the obedient ones of Adam's children. His wisdom made it possible for him to provide this means of restoring the way of life begun in Eden and his almighty power made it certain to be carried out.

OBJECT AND MANNER OF CHRIST'S RETURN

After further study it became clear that Jesus left heaven as a spirit creature, came to earth and became a perfect human being and had to do so in order to become the redeemer.[11] That meant he was not part man and part God.[12] Only by becoming a man as Adam had been could Jesus satisfy the righteous requirements of God's just law on the basis of an eye for an eye, a tooth for a tooth and a life for a life.[13] They learned that when Jesus died as a ransom sacrifice he actually died,[14] but when Jehovah raised him from the dead and he returned to heaven he was given the divine nature or immortality, which he now has.[15]

What a prospect this opened up to them! Now, they realized, when Jesus comes again—and the Bible shows that he will—he is coming as an exalted spirit creature to give to obedient humans the benefits accruing from his sacrifice. That was their conclusion; their joy was unbounded. Young Russell wrote of this joyful awakening in the words of the disciples who encountered Jesus on their way to Emmaus after his resurrection: [16] "Did not our heart burn within us, while he talked with us by the way, and while he opened to us the scriptures?"

But how was Christ Jesus to come? It was during this same period of study, from 1870 to 1876, that they came to recognize the difference between our Lord as "the man who gave himself," and our Lord as he would return, in spirit form. It had become clear to them that spirit creatures could be present, yet invisible; so they could not accept the teachings of the Second Adventists who expected Christ to return in the flesh. These groups were making so many unscriptural predictions as to the object and manner of the Lord's coming, and the things they expected were so fanciful, that they brought great reproach not only on themselves but on all Bible students who were earnestly watching for and proclaiming the coming Kingdom.

Having an unusually logical mind, young Russell would not jump to a conclusion, merely accepting certain premises and theories advanced without foundation. He must have Scriptural support and sound reason. That, of course, excluded the Second Adventists' theories because many of them were unreasoning extremists who believed that when Christ came he would burn up the earth and all people on it except Second Adventists. In a sincere effort to counteract the harmful effect of their erroneous teachings, in 1873 Russell wrote and published at his own personal expense a booklet, *The Object and Manner of Our Lord's Return*. Thousands of copies were distributed.

TIME PROPHECIES SHOW PRESENCE IMMINENT

However, the time features of the Lord's second coming were still somewhat vague to these young Bible students. They realized it was to be soon, but found it impossible to agree with current claims of chronology. Strangely, it was in this very connection that circumstances were again to alter Russell's course and another seemingly insignificant occurrence was to revolutionize his thinking.

At the age of twenty-four, during the winter of 1875–76, Russell went to Philadelphia. His purpose was to open up some men's furnishing stores there and to buy some merchandise, since this was something of a wholesale center at that time. Still fresh in his mind, also, were the many truths that had been revealed to him, uppermost being that of the "restitution of mankind" at the Lord's invisible presence.

One day in January he came to his office and saw a magazine lying on the desk. It was the *Herald of the Morning*. Seeing by the picture on its cover that it was connected with Adventism, he picked it up with some curiosity, saying to himself, "I wonder what idea they have now about the Lord's coming and what the new date is that they have set for the burning up of the earth."

He opened it and, much to his astonishment, observed the conclusion set forth somewhat cautiously that the Lord was already present and that Jesus' illustration of dividing the "wheat" and "tares" in judgment [17] was already in progress.

Russell refused to allow his personal views to dissuade him from investigating. Immediately he wrote to the editor, Nelson H. Barbour, at Rochester, New York, where the magazine was published. He learned enough about Barbour's time calculations to arouse his deep interest. Barbour told him that a reader of *Herald of the Morning* who owned a new Bible translation, *The Emphatic Diaglott*, had noticed a somewhat peculiar variation in the rendering of Matthew 24:3 (as well as verses 27, 37 and 39). Instead of "What shall be the sign of thy *coming*" (as in the common version), this new translation read: "What will be the sign of thy presence." [18] Here was a new thought. Surely if our Lord were to return invisibly to mankind he would give some necessary evidence as to the time of his arrival. This was a reasonable conclusion.

Still Russell wanted convincing proof, and since there were no books explaining these points of chronology he sent at once to Rochester and paid Barbour's expenses to Philadelphia. Here Barbour proceeded to set forth enough proofs from Bible prophecies to convince Russell that the harvest period had begun in 1874.

THE HARVEST MESSAGE BEGINS

Russell was a man of action as well as conviction, and he was fully dedicated to the Lord.

"Mr. Barbour," he said, "the Lord's time is here for us to tell the people about this. The harvest is already two years under way."

"There's no use in doing anything any more," Barbour replied. "The subscribers to the *Herald of the Morning* are discouraged because 1874 has passed and the Lord didn't come. Some of them lived in 1844 with Miller and the Lord didn't come then, and now they've become discouraged. The printing outfit we have in Rochester is about worn out and we're just getting out the *Herald* now and then when we can raise some money. Now there's no use trying to revive it."

Russell was not to be stopped so easily. "Mr. Barbour," he said, "now is the time to get busy; we have something to tell the people—something you never had before."

"What do you mean?"

"We're going to tell them that the time for the harvest is here! We can now carry the good tidings that Christ's kingdom is due to bring to mankind the blessings he purchased for them on Calvary. We've preached restitution before but we have never yet been able to point out that we are living when those blessings are to be restored to mankind. This should be preached on a world-wide scale."

That was Russell's enthusiastic response, and in the years that followed his zeal never diminished.

PREACHING AND PUBLISHING

Immediately he set to work. He gave Barbour some money and authorized him to return to Rochester to begin preparation of a book which they were to co-author. He purposed to set forth for the first time in printed form a Scriptural explanation of the blessings of the restitution combined with the time prophecies of Christ's second presence. This book, *The Three Worlds*, was published in 1877.

Russell now determined to curtail his business and spend his entire time traveling and preaching. It became clear to him at once that, while public lectures aroused interest, something was needed to hold and develop it. To accomplish this he determined to begin active publication of a monthly journal. Although Barbour was acquainted with printing and had been editor of the *Herald* for some years, he raised a number of objections as to the advisability of reorganizing the printing establishment. However, Russell had real enthusiasm for the work and finally it was agreed for Barbour to buy new type and other printing equipment, which Russell himself paid for. So publication of *Herald of the Morning* was resumed, with Barbour as editor and Russell associate editor.

MAINTAINING THE MIND OF THE LORD

Expecting the Lord Jesus to come in 1878 to catch them up miraculously to be with him in heaven, some who had been Second Adventists (including Barbour) were disappointed when that miracle did not occur. Russell, though, "did not for a moment feel cast down," but "realized that what God

had so plainly declared must some time have a fulfillment";
and he "wanted to have it just in God's time and way." [19]

On one occasion while talking with Russell about the events
of 1878, I told him that Pittsburgh papers had reported he was
on the Sixth Street bridge dressed in a white robe on the night
of the Memorial of Christ's death, expecting to be taken to
heaven together with many others. I asked him, "Is that correct?"

Russell laughed heartily and said: "I was in bed that night
between 10:30 and 11:00 P.M. However, some of the more
radical ones might have been there, but I was not. Neither did
I expect to be taken to heaven at that time, for I felt there was
much work to be done preaching the Kingdom message to the
peoples of the earth before the church would be taken away."

It was right at the time of this disappointment, as Russell
shows,[20] that a permanent breach began between Barbour and
Russell. Paul's words at 1 Corinthians 15:51, 52, were being
wrongly construed, Russell had pointed out. There, in Paul's
statement, "We shall not all *sleep*," the word *sleep* is not syn-
onymous with *die*, though some had so understood. Rather,
here *sleep* means state of *unconsciousness* of those who in
death must wait for Christ's second coming to awaken them
out of such *sleep*.[21] Russell showed how Paul clearly meant
by his words that those alive on earth when Christ returned
would not need to go into such *sleep* of death to wait for a
future awakening, but at the instant of their death they then
would be "changed" or resurrected immediately, to be with
Christ in heaven as spirit persons. This harmonizes with Paul's
words in this same chapter, verse 36: "That which thou sow-
est is not quickened, *except it die*."

But Barbour rejected this simple explanation of Paul's words,
feeling that he had to "get up something new to divert attention from the failure of the living saints to be caught away
en masse."

Soon afterward Barbour wrote and published in the *Herald*

"that Christ's death was no more a settlement of the penalty of man's sins than would the sticking of a pin through the body of a fly and causing it suffering and death be considered by an earthly parent as a just settlement for misdemeanor in his child." That denial by Barbour of the basic Bible doctrine of the ransom value of Jesus' sacrifice came as a real shock to Russell.

Russell, who now had been regularly contributing to the *Herald,* immediately wrote and published a powerful defense of the ransom. Then, in the same journal, Barbour and a few supporters continued attacking the ransom doctrine while Russell and others kept on upholding it. *Herald* readers were confused; it also greatly disturbed Russell. To him the ransom was the keystone, the great foundation of human hope. To attack it was to shake the basis of God's provision for reconciling sinful man to himself.

However, Russell soon realized that continued wrangling would not settle the problem. He determined, therefore, to withdraw his support from the *Herald,* to which he himself had given new life in order to preach the good tidings of the harvest work. But just to withdraw, he saw, would not be sufficient. The ransom must be defended and the work of proclaiming our Lord's return must be continued. In July, 1879, the first issue of *Zion's Watch Tower and Herald of Christ's Presence* was published by C. T. Russell.

In 1884 the nonprofit, charitable corporation was chartered that now is known as Watch Tower Bible and Tract Society of Pennsylvania. It has served as the legal and business agent of Jehovah's witnesses ever since.

From these small beginnings a tremendous growth has resulted. The message contained in *The Watchtower* has never halted. From a first distribution of six thousand copies its circulation had grown by 1957 to more than three million copies in forty-six languages. Its message of comfort and hope has assisted an ever-growing host of supporters to change over their thinking and to make straight paths for their feet.[22] By 1957 the number of persons actively engaged in preaching this good news of Jehovah's kingdom had expanded to well over six hundred and fifty thousand.

WHAT BIBLE STUDY REVEALED

Now the issue begun in Eden is to be settled for all time. The good news being preached holds out a prospect of endless life in a world of God's making. You can be sure the way of life begun by God in Eden is not to be lost to mankind. The disobedient act of Adam and Eve has not altered God's purpose. What the first pair did in wrongfully eating of the tree was a little thing, a small happening; but it changed the history of the world. Their yielding to their own personal preference lost for themselves and for their offspring the widest range of individual freedom. It was a corrupting of their minds.[23] Do you think if we persist in their way that it will bring us closer to God? Truth is more important than individuals. It is not a matter of adopting "the religion of your own choice." That is what Adam and Eve did. It is a matter of finding and holding to the one true religion that is God's choice for us.

"Let this mind be in you, which was also in Christ Jesus: ... he humbled himself, and became obedient unto death." [24]

CHAPTER 3

"GOD'S WORD IS A FIRE"

No doubt you have heard some religious observers of Jehovah's witnesses deplore the lack of zeal in their own organizations. They say that if their workers would go from house to house as Jehovah's witnesses do much could be done to stimulate interest in their own way of life.

But is a doorbell-ringing campaign enough to inspire faith?

A man is only as strong physically as the food he eats. Spiritually, then, what gives Jehovah's witnesses the vigor that sends them out to the homes of strangers? Obviously it is their spiritual diet, the same food that invigorates those whom they serve to join them in active worship.

Throughout the centuries Jehovah's witnesses have been impelled by the same active force of God. That which moves them is the message they bear. If their belief were not of sufficient vitality to make them speak, how could it possibly stimulate others to respond? However, the apostle Paul pointed out: [1] "I planted, Apollos watered, but God kept making it grow." This is the growth to which Jehovah's witnesses accredit their increase.

THE IDENTIFYING TAG

Shortly after publication in 1886 of C. T. Russell's first *Millennial Dawn* volume, *The Plan of the Ages*, a convention had been arranged for Allegheny, Pennsylvania, on the occasion of the annual Memorial celebration of Christ's death. In those early days at our conventions it was customary to have a meeting at which different ones present would rise and give what we called a testimony. On this particular occasion Russell himself had charge of the meeting and was encouraging new ones from other cities present to join in the expressions. He was getting a ready enough response from some of the regular attenders but none of the visiting friends were inclined to volunteer, and yet there were a number of new ones present.

After the meeting had been in progress for some time an elderly man poked his head in the doorway at the rear of the hall, looked around, then straightened up and walked in. Although there were still a few seats at the rear, he struck out for the front row and that's where he sat down. Russell looked at him. He bore unmistakable marks of a traveler who had come from some distance. His clothes were quite dusty and with him he had a small package of personal belongings that he deposited carefully under his seat. For a while he sat quietly, listening to the various testimonies. Then finally he got up.

The chairman wondered, "Now what is he going to say?" But having called for comments from visitors, he thought,

"Well, this is the Lord's meeting, so we'll give him a chance."

He did not have long to wait.

"Well, I'm here!" the stranger began. That brought a laugh. The fact was obvious; but the old fellow wanted everyone to realize he was glad to be there.

"Now I'm not going to say much," he continued, "but I just arrived in town. I came down from New England and I had to change trains up the road here a piece. I had about an hour, so I thought I'd hand out a few tracts to the people on the platform. I noticed some men standing around a platform truck and they were all laughing; so I walked over to them.

" 'What's all the excitement?' I asked.

"They pointed to a goat in a crate on the truck.

" 'What's wrong with the goat?'

" 'Nothing. They just don't know where to send him, that's all.'

" 'Well, doesn't he have a tag on him?'

" 'He had a tag when he started out; but he got hungry and ate it up. Now they don't know what to do with him.'

"Now, folks," the old fellow continued to the audience, "my name's George M. Kellogg. I'm a deacon in the Presbyterian Church and now I'm like that goat. I got a copy of this book and read it (here he drew out of his pocket a copy of *The Plan of the Ages*, holding it up), and I'm like that goat. At one time I had a tag but I ate it up and now I don't know where I belong; so I came here because I want to find out."

That was all it took to get them started. Stirred by Kellogg's remarks many of the visitors stood up as opportunity afforded and said they were in the same position. They were Methodists, Baptists and Presbyterians, but their tags were gone too and they would like to know where they belonged. Before the convention was over they all found out and Kellogg, for one, lived for a number of years as a faithful minister in Jehovah's service.

EARLY BACKGROUND

Like Charles Russell, my own association with the work began in my youth, as I've already mentioned. I, too, was seeking a way to serve God in an acceptable manner, and, though my first acquaintance with the doctrines and work of Jehovah's witnesses brought me much joy, it required a real change-over in my thinking.

I was born July 2, 1877, in Canada. Both my parents were strict Presbyterians and active church members. However, I was brought up in a Catholic community in Nova Scotia where there was no Protestant church, just a Catholic church. We did have a hall in town where we had Sunday school and prayer meetings, and that was the extent of our religious activities. It was three or four miles out to the regular Presbyterian church, and when we attended church that is where we would go. As a youngster I did not study much about things of the Bible but I had a reverential attitude toward church matters. I accepted what my father and mother told me as true.

My oldest brother was a skeptic and finally shocked us boys greatly by admitting privately he was an agnostic. He said: "If there is a God then he's something different from what the Calvinists say he is. I don't believe what they teach about predestination. If God assigned some humans to eternal torment and others to heavenly glory before they were born, where is there any justice? Then they tell us those in heaven sing God's praises and that's why he takes them there—because he enjoys that. But they also say those in hell-fire are there because it's God's pleasure. All I can say is he must enjoy the groans of those suffering in hell more than he enjoys the singing of those in heaven because he is taking only a little flock to heaven but they claim he has sent billions to hell. I can't believe in such a God." That horrified me.

A FAMILY TRAGEDY

I never became active about my religion until a real tragedy
occurred in our family. One winter when I was about thirteen my younger sister and I were out on a Saturday with our
hand sleds, coasting. We got overheated. The next morning
my little sister came down with diphtheria. They called it
membranous croup.

Monday evening she was dead.

This came as a great shock to me. I said, "Life is short and
uncertain. If what we do here has any bearing on what we
will be hereafter, then we would be very foolish if we didn't
devote our time to serving the Lord now with the hope of
having something better throughout eternity. As for me, I'm
going to take my stand and do what I think will be pleasing
to the Lord."

In our town there were only a few Protestant boys and they
did not understand why I got so religious all at once. Nevertheless, I held on and did the best I could to serve the Lord
as we understood it in my church.

RELIGIOUS AMBITIONS

When I reached the age of sixteen I decided to be a preacher.
I went away to school some distance from home, preparatory
to attending a theological seminary. For some reason not clear
to me now I suffered a nervous breakdown and had to quit.
I came home discouraged and almost brokenhearted, not
knowing what to do. However, my father was very considerate and kind and did not reprimand me in any way but
offered to do anything he could for me. I obtained some
money from him and went away to Boston, Massachusetts.

Alone in that large city, I was uncertain indeed as to the

future. But I intended to look around to see what I could find in the way of a religious life.

I had not been there long until Dwight L. Moody and his associates Ira David Sankey, Francis Murphy and Sam Jones came to town to hold a revival. For about two weeks Moody spoke twice a day in the Tremont Temple and it was a truly exciting experience to me to see such large crowds coming to church. Their idea was to "surrender yourself to God" and be saved by his grace.

How well I remember the turmoil in my young mind as I tried seriously to consider all of the consequences of such a responsible act. One night I lay awake until after midnight, tossing and turning, trying to tear my mind free of the prospect of all the natural pleasures of life. I was by nature a happy sort of person, and laughter and joking were as much a part of me as breathing. Would I have to give up these things, I thought? Religion and a religious life had always been painted to me as one of austerity, with a long-faced pious attitude that would not tolerate much levity. I was told Jesus never laughed, but he often wept. Still I knew that I could not be truly happy unless I could be serving God in some way.

That night is as clear in my mind as if it were yesterday. Finally I made up my mind. I got down on my knees and "surrendered" myself to God. I know now that was one of the most important acts of my life and since then I have never had cause to regret it. I did not experience a great flash of light coming on me but I know that from that night forward I have grown steadily in understanding and appreciation of what it means to serve God. I have learned, too, that my previous notions as to what it meant to be "serious" about religion were all wrong. I have never lost my sense of humor.

I made up my mind then, saying, "Now I know definitely what I'm going to do. I'm going to be a missionary of some kind if I can't become a regular minister." So I planned to go

to the Moody School at Northfield, Massachusetts, and study
to be a missionary.

Not long after this and before I could make arrangements to
attend the Moody School, I was discussing religion with some
of the men in the commission house where we were working.
A middle-aged man came in, listened to us a minute, and then
joined in the conversation. I could see that he knew more than
I did about the Bible, so I inquired where he got his information. He invited me to come to a meeting at No. 4 Park Square
in Boston, at 3:30 P.M. the next Sunday. I accepted.

The speaker at that meeting, Alexander M. Graham, was
giving a talk on the progressive ages of man's history in his
relation to God. I could not follow him too well because the
material was new to me. He talked fast and I did not have
time to consider the meaning of all the figures, lines and curves
on the chart he was using to illustrate his talk. However, I
enjoyed the meeting; but, more important, there I obtained
the first *Millennial Dawn* book, *The Plan of the Ages*.

That very night I began to read. The first chapter quoted
Psalm 30:5—"Weeping may endure for a night, but joy
cometh in the morning." The writer (whose identity was un-
known to me at the time, for the book did not contain his
name) described briefly the sufferings of humanity for the
past six thousand years; he pointed to the morning of a new
day at hand.

"Well, that sounds like the truth!" I thought. "That's reasonable; that's what I want; that's Godlike. This will answer
my questions as to man's destiny and God's purpose for man's
being on earth."

In the next chapter proof was submitted that there is a God;
another viewed the Bible as a divine revelation in the light of

reason. Next, epochs or dispensations of the world's history were explained and the main outlines of the "three worlds" given.

Chapter 5, entitled "The Hidden Mystery," cleared up a question I had never been able to understand: Why are efforts of the church to convert the world making so little progress? The matter of man's salvation was of deep concern to me. In Chapter 5 this was explained. Centuries ago, as recorded in the Bible, God had promised his faithful witness Abraham that he would bless all the families of earth through Abraham's seed.[2] But who was that Seed? I didn't know. Here it was explained that Jesus Christ and his bride, the true church, was the Seed.[3] Furthermore, that Seed would not be completed until all members of the true church had been gathered in the final harvest. Since that harvest was still going on it was not yet time to bring the promised blessings to the faithful ones of mankind.

"HIS WORD A BURNING FIRE"

Now it was clear to me why the world was not being converted, and what else was necessary before mankind in general would be restored to a peaceful way of life. I was so happy about this that I literally could not contain myself. I would go out on the street and stop people to tell them what I had learned.

Today many, especially relatives and friends, cannot understand why it is that, when one becomes really acquainted with the work of Jehovah's witnesses and accepts Bible truths and begins to preach them, he sometimes appears to be a little extreme at first. Perhaps that has been your own experience with one of Jehovah's witnesses. Well, persons who are happy about anything seldom are quiet about it. They generally are very expressive, showing their joy. They want everyone else to share it.

So, when one really sees from the Bible the glorious picture of the blessings God has promised obedient human beings during the thousand-year reign of Jesus Christ just ahead, he does not want to keep it to himself. He has to go out and tell others about it, especially those who are near and dear to him. It reminds me of what the prophet Jeremiah of old said when he deliberately tried to keep quiet about the message he had been given to proclaim,[4] "His word was in mine heart as a burning fire shut up in my bones, and I was weary with forbearing, and I could not stay." That is exactly the way I felt when I learned about the promised blessings for all families of earth through Abraham's seed.

One day, as I recall, I approached a stranger on the street. Without any other greeting I asked him, "Do you know about the great promise God made to Abraham, that through his seed all the families of the earth would be blessed?"

Looking at me in surprise, the man asked, "What Abraham are you talking about?—the Abraham that has that pawn shop down on Salem Street?"

That was all the interest he had in my message. I'll never forget how disappointed I was at his reaction. True, I still was quite young, but the blessing of mankind was to me at that time the most important matter I could think of. However, I was not discouraged by this man's seeming lack of interest. I continued talking to anyone who would listen. Later, of course, I learned a more tactful and less startling approach.

Then I almost lost all I had gained.

STUMBLED BY TRADITION

A short time before all this a number of prominent clergymen, including G. Campbell Morgan, had come to Boston to carry

on a religious campaign. They were connected with the Moody
School at Northfield. Some of their talks were exposing teachings of the Unitarians. The Unitarians did not believe that
Jesus had a pre-human existence or that he was the redeemer
of mankind. To them he was just a remarkable man who set a
good example to be followed.

I had attended many of the campaign meetings held by those
clergymen. They were fluent speakers. They told many stories that were designed to attract and interest the unlearned.
I recall one of them said: "All of the apostles called Jesus
'Lord' but Judas; he called him 'Rabbi.' . . . Oh well," the
speaker added, "Judas was a Unitarian and that's why he did
that." This had impressed my youthful mind because I certainly did not want to be like Judas. These thoughts were still
in my mind as I continued reading my precious book, *The
Plan of the Ages.*

I came to its Chapter 10: "Spiritual and Human Natures
Separate and Distinct." There I read this statement: [5]

> We are told that Jesus, before becoming a man (in his pre-
> human existence), was "in a form of God"—a spiritual form,
> a spirit being; but since to be a ransom for mankind, he must
> be a man, of the same nature of the sinner whose substitute in
> death he was to become, it was therefore necessary that his
> nature be changed; and Paul tells us that he took not the na-
> ture of angels, one step lower than his own, but came down
> two steps, and took the nature of men—he became a man; he
> was "made flesh." [6]

Jesus nothing more than a perfect man on earth? That statement left me confused. I was greatly shocked. Violently I
threw the book to the other end of my room, saying to myself,
"I'm certainly not going to be a Unitarian, but the author of
this book must be!"

"MADE IN THE LIKENESS OF MEN"

For a few moments I sat there in serious thought. I felt depressed, and finally concluded, "I've lost something that was very precious and dear to me. That book brought me more joy and peace and satisfaction than anything I have come in contact with. Now why throw it away because of the one point that I can't understand? Should I allow something that some men have said prevent me from considering the evidences, at least?" (Of course I learned later that C. T. Russell had no connection with the Unitarians.)

I walked across the room and took the book up from under the table where I had thrown it, dusted it off and began to read it all over again. Then I saw *why* Jesus had to become a man. It was in order to meet the terms of the sentence God had pronounced against the perfect man Adam. The perfect Adam had brought the curse of death upon all his offspring; for any to be redeemed it would require a perfect man's sacrifice. Jesus could accomplish this only by becoming a man.

Now that was reasonable, I thought. Just assuming the form of a man while retaining his spirit nature would not answer God's law of an eye for an eye, a life for a life. Besides, if he were part God all this time, what must he have been thinking for the nine months he was in Mary's womb, or for the time he was growing from infancy to manhood? Certainly he was not just acting a part all those years. That would have made him a hypocrite. Yet if he were really God, then he must have been conscious of more than a real child; otherwise God is no different from men.

Now I could see what Paul meant when he wrote [7] that Jesus "took upon him the form of a servant, and was made in the likeness of men." Realizing, too, that there is a legal basis for the hope God has given us, it makes even stronger our certainty that the God who cannot deny himself will carry it out. The joy that this understanding brought me has not diminished with the passing years. From that day to this I have never had any difficulty in understanding and appreciating any of the points of doctrine that have been revealed relative to the redemptive work of Jesus, the resurrection and the restoration of the way of life begun in Eden.

FIRE NOT LITERAL

At that time I was a member of the Tremont Temple in Boston and we had there a Bible class of some two hundred young men and women. Many spent more time socializing than they did in studying, but to me it was really an opportunity to gain more knowledge of the Bible.

One Sunday we were considering the parable of the sheep and goats for our Sunday school lesson. Mr. Jamison, a broker down on State Street, was leading the study. He was talking about the goats' being cast off into the fire of eternal torment as he summed up the lesson.

When he had finished, I got up and said, "Mr. Jamison, I would like to ask a question. If the goats and the sheep in this parable are just symbols of human creatures, the sheep of good people and the goats of wicked ones, then why do you say that the fire is literal and that the goats are going to be tormented forever?"

He turned around to the class and shook his finger at me and said: "That young man by that question has destroyed in this class all the good I've done teaching during the whole quarter."

That was an indication to stay away, and I did; although there were a few who felt the question was a reasonable one and wanted to discuss it with me further. From that time on I began to attend meetings at the Park Square hall where I had obtained the book, *The Plan of the Ages*. I continued to study there and to engage in the work that was available to us at that time.

C. T. RUSSELL GREETS A YOUTH

Next summer saw the turn of the century and I met Pastor Russell. It was at a convention in Philadelphia. June 17 was Bunker Hill day in Massachusetts and, of course, a holiday. There were special train rates to Philadelphia at that time because the Republican party was also holding a convention there. That year they nominated William McKinley as president and Theodore Roosevelt vice-president of the United States. So I took advantage of the holiday and special rates and went to the Bible students' convention sponsored by the Watch Tower Bible and Tract Society. There, as I now recall, Russell talked to the public on the subject, "Salvation from what, to what?" The theme of his discourse was that men are not saved from eternal torment, which does not exist. They are saved from eternal death to everlasting life.

After the talk I was delighted to meet the speaker. He was an extremely kind man. I was just about the only young person there. All others present seemed mature in years. His willingness to talk to me impressed me greatly, because I knew of no man of his importance on the public platform who would talk face to face with young people from his audience after his lectures. I recall that in Boston Dwight L. Moody would leave the hall immediately after his sermons and go to his hotel nearby. Anyone who desired to ask questions would have to go to others of Moody's party. But C. T. Russell always made himself personally available to anyone who wished to talk to him.

INVITATION TO HEADQUARTERS

From that time I never missed any convention that was held in the East or the Middle West. In September, 1900, after returning from Philadelphia to Boston, I was baptized by total immersion in water, the service being conducted by Hayden Samson, a traveling representative of the Society. In July, 1901, I was ready to realize my ambition to become a missionary and entered the full-time ministry in Massachusetts.

In September of that year we had a convention in Cleveland and I attended. It was at this time that President McKinley was assassinated at the Pan-American Exposition in Buffalo, New York, so there was much excitement throughout the country. The convention at Cleveland ended Sunday night and Russell invited me to make my home at the Watch Tower Society's headquarters in Allegheny, though I was not a member of the staff. When I went there to the Bible House (where the headquarters "family" lived and worked) I was in my early twenties. C. T. Russell was very kind to me. I had no home, both my parents having died; so he took me under his wing and made me feel at home with the headquarters family. He was thoughtful and considerate in every way, and as I would go out on a trip or special assignment he always would say, "Brother, the door is open for you when you return. This is your home."

In October, 1902, I attended a convention in Washington, D.C., where I was married. My wife and I then spent a year in California, returning in 1904 to Allegheny. In 1905 I made a nation-wide convention tour with Russell. It was on this trip that I met J. F. Rutherford, whom I baptized in 1906 and who became the second president of the Society.

In 1909, due to expansion of the organization world-wide, headquarters were moved from Allegheny to Brooklyn, New York. There, at 13–17 Hicks Street, a mission annex of the Plymouth Congregational Church, called "Plymouth Bethel," was purchased and new operating offices of the Society were installed and a large auditorium utilized for meetings. The building was called the "Brooklyn Tabernacle."

At the same time the former residence of the Plymouth church's famous preacher, Henry Ward Beecher, was purchased. This was at 124 Columbia Heights. Here the head-quarters family were housed and the structure was named "Bethel," supplanting the term "Bible House" used for the Society's building in Allegheny. International headquarters of the Society and the headquarters family are still at this address and, after all these years, I am still a happy member of that family.

DARKNESS LIGHTENING INTO DAY

As I consider the years that I have been associated with the organization of Jehovah's witnesses I can appreciate more and more the value of the path along which we have been led by Jehovah God. Until I first began to study I had never been able to find any religious teaching that answered all my questions. And yet the knowledge of God's Word that was available to us at that time was so limited (compared with what we now rejoice in) that it would be like coming out of the faint light of dawn into the brightness of high noon. But the gradual growth in knowledge, as well as in numbers of persons associating in the work, has strengthened and developed the organization and brought it to maturity.

C. T. Russell had no idea of building a strongly knit organization. At that time we saw no need for it. We expected 1914 would mark the end of this system of things on earth. Our big concern at that time was to preach as effectively and extensively as possible before that date arrived. In the meantime, we thought, we must prepare ourselves individually to be ready to go to heaven.

Exactly what would occur in 1914 we did not then know, but of one thing we were certain: The year 1914 would see the beginning of the worst time of trouble the earth had yet known; for so many Bible prophecies foretold that. Our faith was strong and our hopes were based on much more than mere

human speculation. Yet 1914 and the years that immediately
followed proved to be a time of severe testing for the developing New World society. Had we realized then the trials we
were still to face or the years that were to elapse before our
preaching commission was due to expire, perhaps we would
have entered the year with far more agitation of mind.

4

"END OF ALL KINGDOMS IN 1914"

THE YEAR 1914 is marked for all time to come. On our hope's horizon, for months, yes, years, that date had loomed ahead of us. We had viewed it with constantly increasing expectancy. So much was to be realized, yet so many things were to be feared. Time prophecies of the Bible had been checked and rechecked. We did not doubt them. Still, we knew this date would usher in the worst time of trouble the world had yet known. Would we be able to survive?

Opinions as to what, exactly, was to occur varied. Of course *The Watch Tower* had stated the matter rather clearly, but at that time there was far more independent thinking and private "interpretation" than the Scriptures themselves allow for. This was one lesson we were yet to learn and our experiences during this time of crisis did much to clear our thinking and understanding as to what constitutes private interpretation. I certainly have reason to recognize its dangers.

Ever since 1879 *The Watch Tower* had been calling attention to the foretold end of the present systems as due to begin in 1914. But while we were all looking forward to 1914 and the end of wickedness and sorrow in the earth, many of us were thinking more of our own personal, individual "change" than anything else.

On August 23, 1914, as I well recall, Pastor Russell started on a trip to the Northwest, down the Pacific coast and over into the Southern states, and then ending at Saratoga Springs, New York, where we held a convention September 27–30. That was a highly interesting time because a few of us seriously thought we were going to heaven during the first week of that October.

At that Saratoga Springs convention quite a number were in attendance. Wednesday (September 30) I was invited to talk on the subject, "The End of All Things Is at Hand; Therefore Let Us Be Sober, Watchful and Pray." Well, as one would say, that was down my road. I believed it myself sincerely—that the church was "going home" in October. During that discourse I made this unfortunate remark: "This is probably the last public address I shall ever deliver because we shall be going home soon."

Next morning (October 1) about five hundred of us began the return trip to Brooklyn, including a lovely ride on the Hudson River Day Line steamer from Albany to New York. Sunday morning we were to open services in Brooklyn, this to conclude our convention.

Quite a number of the conventioners stayed at Bethel, the home of the headquarters staff members. Friday morning (October 2) we all were seated at the breakfast table when Russell came down. As he entered the room he hesitated a moment as was his custom and said cheerily, "Good morning, all." But this morning, instead of proceeding to his seat as usual, he briskly clapped his hands and happily announced: "The Gentile times have ended; their kings have had their day." We all applauded.

We were highly excited and I would not have been surprised if at that moment we had just started up, that becoming
the signal to begin ascending heavenward—but of course there
was nothing like that, really.

Russell took his seat at the head of the table and made a few
remarks, and then I came in for some good-natured twitting.
He said, "We are going to make some changes in the program
for Sunday. At 10:30 Sunday morning Brother Macmillan
will give us an address." Everybody laughed heartily, recalling what I had said on Wednesday at Saratoga Springs—my
"last public address"!

Well, then I had to get busy to find something to say. I
found Psalm 74:9, "We see not our signs: there is no more any
prophet: neither is there among us any that knoweth how
long." Now that was different. In that talk I tried to show the
friends that perhaps some of us had been a bit too hasty in
thinking that we were going to heaven right away, and the
thing for us to do would be to keep busy in the Lord's service
until he determined when any of his approved servants would
be taken home to heaven.

"THE WRONG THING AT THE RIGHT TIME"

This had been exactly the view of C. T. Russell all along. He
had observed with considerable disgust the fantastic predictions of some of the extremists among the Second Adventists
who had brought upon themselves and all other sincere students of the Bible unnecessary reproach from those not sufficiently informed to see the difference. Time after time their
predictions had proved false, and some of the groups began to
disintegrate through continued disappointments.

As 1914 approached, we, too, were expecting the end. But
when that date arrived and we did not go to heaven, did
things end for us? When it appeared that not all events ex-

pected for 1914 were to materialize that year, did we fall apart? Did we lose sight of our hope? Was the confident voice of *The Watch Tower* silenced? No! Why? Well, this is the way C. T. Russell put it even as the year 1914 was just beginning: [1]

If later it should be demonstrated that the Church is not glorified by October, 1914, we shall try to feel content with whatever the Lord's will may be. . . . We believe that the chronology is a blessing. If it should wake us . . . earlier in the Morning than we would otherwise have waked, *well and good!* It is those who are *awake* who get the *blessing.* . . . If in the Lord's providence the time should come *twenty-five years later,* then that would be our will. This would not change the fact that the Son of God was sent by the Father, and that the Son is the Redeemer of our race; that He died for our sins; that He is selecting the Church for His Bride; and that the next thing now in order is the establishment of the glorious Kingdom at the hands of this great Mediator, who . . . will bless all the families of the earth. . . . If October, 1915, should pass, and we should find ourselves still here and matters going on very much as they are at present, . . . then we would think, Have we been expecting the wrong thing at the right time? The Lord's will *might* permit this.

Russell was not confused on the major events due to take place. He recognized that whether the individual members of the spiritual "little flock" were left on earth or not it would not alter or affect the time schedule for bringing an end to the nations' uninterrupted rule. That is why he emphasized "the next thing now in order is the establishment of the glorious Kingdom at the hands of this great Mediator," the Son of God, Jesus Christ. This, he knew, must occur when "the Gentile times have ended," and that is what he wished to emphasize.

Russell did not say without good reason in October of 1914 that "the Gentile times have ended." Many years before this he had published information which clearly developed Jesus' statement,[2] "Jerusalem shall be trodden down of the Gentiles, until the times of the Gentiles be fulfilled." He pointed out that this term "the times of the Gentiles" applied to the period beginning with the time that kings ceased to rule in God's typical theocratic nation of Israel and ending with the setting up of Jesus Christ as the rightful King of the whole world. He said this period began in the year 607 B.C. and was due to end A.D. 1914.

Here is the way the chronology was determined:

King David, first of the Judean kings of Israel, was said to sit "on the throne of Jehovah." [3] His dynasty thus continued theocratic rule until it was overthrown in the days of Zedekiah at the destruction of Jerusalem.[4] This date is reckoned from secular and Biblical history as the fall of 607 B.C.[5] At that time it was foretold that the theocratic line of Israel's kings would be interrupted until he came "whose right it is." [6] In view of Jerusalem's capture by a pagan king this would infer a period of rule by Gentiles until the time for God to set up his own Kingdom.[7] Jesus, during his first advent, spoke of these "times of the Gentiles" and indicated they would expire at his return or second advent.[8] If it could be determined how long the "times of the Gentiles" were to last, then the time for Christ's return and the setting up of his kingdom would be known as a certainty.

Now, of course, the date 1914 itself is not given in the Bible. Neither was the date of Jesus' first advent, for that matter, yet the Jews were expecting him.[9] Just so, the length of the period referred to as the "times of the Gentiles" is indicated in the Bible but it is given in symbolic language. Foretelling a temporary period of insanity for Jerusalem's captor, Nebuchadnezzar, because of his high-handed disregard of Jehovah's rule, the prophecy says: [10] "They shall make thee to eat grass as oxen, and seven times shall pass over thee, until thou know that the most High ruleth in the kingdom of men, and giveth it to whomsoever he will."

This prophecy was literally fulfilled upon Nebuchadnezzar as a symbol of the rule of the nations. When the time expired his kingdom was restored to him and he recognized the supremacy of Jehovah. That is why the restoration of theocratic rule in the hands of Jesus Christ was to be expected at the end of the "Gentile times" and after "seven times" had elapsed. The clue for the length of this period is given at Revelation 12:6, 14 in connection with another prophecy though not related to this one. There, 1,260 days are shown to equal "a time, and times, and half a time." This must be figured as "one time, plus two times, plus one-half time" or three and one-half times, since another unrelated prophecy at Revelation 11:2, 3 shows 1,260 days as 42 months, which is obviously three and one-half years of 360 days each. On this basis, "seven times" would be twice 1,260 days, or 2,520 days.

If the prophecy of Daniel were figured literally as applied to the "Gentile times" then the "seven times" would be only seven years and would have expired long before Jesus' first advent, yet as we have seen, he spoke of the times of the Gentiles as still carrying on. How, then, is this period to be figured?

On two different occasions at least, in the matter of judgment, Jehovah used a day to represent a year.[11] Following this pattern, 2,520 days in the prophecy become 2,520 years in the fulfillment. If the length of time of uninterrupted Gentile rule of earth's nations was to be 2,520 years, then the period would run from the fall of 607 B.C. to A.D. 1914. On the basis of this chronology, the time of Christ's second presence and the beginning of his kingdom rule was confidently expected in the fall of A.D. 1914, and Russell was prompted to announce confidently in October, 1914, "The Gentile times have ended; their kings have had their day."

END OF THE WORLD DOES NOT END WORK

Believing so thoroughly that 1914 marked the end, some of us were assuming that it also marked the time when the church would be "translated." But the Scriptures did not say that, as Russell had tried to suggest to us. Prophecies of the Bible said the nations' uninterrupted rule of the earth would come to a close and Jehovah's kingdom under Christ Jesus would begin to operate at the end of Gentile times, but we have since learned that many other things must occur before the last member of the spiritual "little flock" would finish his earthly course.

That is why Russell wrote as he did in January, 1914, warning us that events might continue for some time after the expected beginning of trouble in the fall of the year. Although many of us still thought we would leave this earth, at least by October of 1915, Russell, who was a good reasoner, saw that there was too much work yet to be done by Jehovah's enlightened people on earth. Again he pointed to the Bible for a careful study of the declared purposes of Jehovah.

Russell's comments on Psalm 149:5–9, as published in May of 1914, show further his desire not to walk ahead of Jehovah's direction and his efforts to encourage us to that same course. The Psalm reads:

"Let the saints be joyful in glory: let them sing aloud upon their beds. Let the high praises of God be in their mouth, and a two-edged sword in their hand."

Russell wrote: [12] "Heretofore we had not questioned that this description of the glory of the saints applied to them beyond the veil (i.e., in heaven)—beyond the completion of the First Resurrection. But a more careful investigation of the words forewarns us that we may not be too sure in such a supposition. We suggest as a bare possibility that a time may

come when a part of the saints will be in glory beyond the
veil, and when those on this side of the veil in the flesh will enter
very fully into the joys of their Lord and into participation in
His work. . . . But the word *beds* here, in harmony with usage
elsewhere in the Bible, would signify a rest of faith—that these
saints were at rest in the midst of conditions to the contrary.
. . . Again, . . . they have the two-edged sword in their hand,
according to the prophecy. This 'two-edged sword' is evidently, as elsewhere, the Word of God. We can scarcely
imagine the saints beyond the veil as handling the Word of
God. . . . On the contrary, this would seem to imply that the
saints described are on this side of the veil, using the Sword of
the Spirit, which is the Word of God, . . . clearing His name
from the dishonor attached to it through the ignorance, super-
stition and creeds of the Dark Ages."

Little did I dream in 1914 when I read those words in *The
Watch Tower* that over forty years later I would still be here
on earth associated with hundreds of thousands of others in
preaching the good news that God's kingdom did begin in
1914 and that the climax was to arrive in our own generation.[13]
Had I realized then what I know now I would not have made
that "last public address" remark at the 1914 Saratoga Springs
convention. How many public addresses I have given since
then I'm sure I can't remember.

Yet here, as early as the spring of 1914, Russell was describ-
ing the work that actually has become a part of the present-
day history of Jehovah's witnesses. He recognized that at least
some members of the anointed "little flock" might remain on
earth to participate in the vindication of the name of Jehovah.
Although at that time he could not foresee all that would take
place, he vividly realized that the end of all Bible-preaching
activity on earth could not come during 1914—after he had
restudied Psalm 149, as indicated above.

RUSSELL FORESEES A POST-WAR EXPANSION

On this point I had an experience with Russell that ever since has kept me constantly enthusiastic about the continuous expansion of this Kingdom-preaching work. It was an interview I had with him a short time before his death in 1916. He pictured the work spreading out much as we see it today, small groups or congregations working independently of the headquarters as far as meetings are concerned, but all working as part of one unified organization. He discussed the matter at length, and although his concern seemed to be primarily with New York City I could glean from his description that he expected the arrangement would likely spread over the whole world.

So it is that we realize that Jehovah has never revealed all his purpose at one time to any of his witnesses, ancient or modern. Knowledge and understanding of the establishing of the kingdom in heaven and of its operation in earth has come gradually—as the rising of the morning sun. The witnesses of Jehovah walk by faith, not by sight. Jehovah reveals to them only such information as they need to equip them to carry on the particular work to which they are assigned for that time.

If there was any question in our minds before 1914 that Jehovah God was directing the affairs of the Watch Tower Society, the events that began that year have thoroughly dispelled such doubts. Says an ancient maxim: [14] "Hope deferred makes the heart sick, but a desire fulfilled is a tree of life." So it has proved to us.

Instead of our organization withering away because some expected things did not materialize, those of us who had not received the clearest possible view of things tightened our spiritual belts, took a prayerful view of the Scriptures to determine our mistake and continued to advance in knowledge and understanding of God's purposes. Since our hope was

based on something real it remained firm and unshaken. This
has been a lesson well learned.

A MAJOR FULFILLMENT OBSCURED BY DETAILS

Jehovah's witnesses expected the "End of All Kingdoms in
1914." We were not disappointed.

At first it looked as if we might come in for real recognition
on the part of some leading observers. A foremost American
newspaper [15] of that time (in its Sunday issue with front-page
headline: "Germans Now Only 70 Miles from Paris") carried
a special article entitled: "End of All Kingdoms in 1914 'Millennial Dawners'' 25-Year Prophecy." The article stated in
part:

> The terrific war outbreak in Europe has fulfilled an ex-
> traordinary prophecy. For a quarter of a century past,
> through preachers and through press, the "International Bible
> Students," best known as "Millennial Dawners," have been
> proclaiming to the world that the Day of Wrath prophesied
> in the Bible would dawn in 1914. . . .
> Rev. Charles T. Russell is the man who has been pro-
> pounding this interpretation of the Scriptures since 1874. . . .
> His surmises have seemed to the average person of no more
> importance than a mystic's dream. And yet on the date set
> we are in the midst of a world-wide war.

However, even such limited popular recognition was short-
lived. As 1914 passed, then 1915 and 1916, the reproach
heaped upon us increased. In our effort to discern the meaning
of Bible prophecy before the expected events had actually occurred, I admit some partially inaccurate public expressions
were made. But when these minor details did not develop, the
more important major fulfillment that actually did occur was
entirely overlooked by those lacking full faith in God's Word.
Instead of viewing the increasing number of facts, actual

events, piling up world-wide from day to day since 1914 as undeniable proof of the correctness of the marked date publicized by *The Watch Tower* from 1879, scoffers seized upon some minor point of Russell's writings to ridicule and mock. Russell concluded: [16] "Our thought is that we should look for still further evidences . . . that God's kingdom has begun its work."

THE TURNING-POINT AT 1914

What have events since 1914 revealed? Do they show we were justified in our persistent preaching for decades before 1914 that a great time of trouble was due to begin in that year? Aside from the question as to how long that period of greatest trouble was to last, what are the facts since the beginning of World War I in the summer of 1914?

A marked year indeed was 1914!

As informed, sober-minded persons now look back to it, they admit that there has been no year like it in man's history. Its unprecedented events will never be repeated.

That 1914 marked the end of an era was openly admitted forty years later by an outstanding American newspaper editor, who wrote: [17] "The last completely 'normal' year in history was 1913, the year before World War I began."

A famed scientist, one of the creators of the atom bomb, in 1951 said: [18] "We have not had a peaceful world since 1914."

But the new era was the beginning of far more than just the atomic age. An associate professor of history at Columbia University wrote: [19] "It is indeed the year 1914 rather than that of Hiroshima which marks the turning point in our time, for by now we can see that, whatever the future may hold in store, it was the first world war that ushered in the era of confused transition in the midst of which we are floundering."

Another newspaper editor recently commented: [20] "It seems

likely that when the history of the twentieth century is written, August 4, 1914, the day hostilities became general in Europe, will loom larger than even the date of the outbreak of the Second World War or the dropping of the first atomic bomb. That August day, we are beginning to realize, marked a dividing line in history. An era of peace, progress and security ended, and an age of war and revolution began."

This view was taken by another leading journalist in making a comparison of the two world wars: [21] "The first war marked a far greater change in history. It closed a long era of general peace and began a new age of violence in which the second war is simply an episode. Since 1914 the world has had a new character: a character of international anarchy. . . . Thus the first World War marks a turning point in modern history."

Another competent observer said: [22] "Forty years ago the world overnight goose-stepped from the 'golden age' into a volcanic epoch marked by bloody wars." And the noted British author, Bertrand Russell, remarked: "Ever since 1914 the world has been reeling drunkenly toward disaster."

Those of you who have lived through this period will no doubt add your own personal testimony to the unmistakable trend in human history since 1914. To deny the change is to ignore the facts.

RUSSELL RECOGNIZES THE RISING COMMUNIST THREAT

In 1879 the new *Watch Tower* magazine's twenty-seven-year-old editor, Charles T. Russell, clearly recognized that there would be a rapid increase in violence, world-wide, and realized its outcome. In that journal's third issue his remarkable discernment of this growing threat was described in these words: [23]

Very many Scriptures seem to teach that the kingdoms of earth will be overthrown by a rising of the people: goaded to desperation from lack of employment and seeking relief from the oppression of bloodthirsty governments. Such a rising and overturning Socialists, Communists and Nihilists of to-day would gladly bring about if they could. . . . And it is astonishing how very rapidly these things once looked at as absurd and impossible are becoming realities. When we with a few others declared these things only a short time since, and called attention to the fact that trouble was taught to be occasioned by a rising of the people and the overthrow of governments—Communism—we were laughed at; there was truly little sign then of Communism; but today every civilized nation is in dread, and Nihilism, Communism and Socialism are household words, and we see "men's hearts failing them for fear and for looking after those things coming on the earth, for the powers of heaven [governments] shall be shaken." (Luke 21:26)

The Communist uprising, according to this 1879 description, was due to begin in 1914 or shortly thereafter, and the dreaded storm's climax was expected to follow immediately. The First World War and the resulting 1917 Bolshevist Revolution in Russia did become the world-shaking event envisioned by Russell almost forty years before. But the final outcome has not yet been seen. After the tremendously turbulent decades of 1914 to 1954, the 1953 death of the Soviet dictator Stalin has seemed to be leading toward a gradual settling—a continuing period of globe-encircling social revolution. Is anyone on earth today unmindful of the immeasurable power of what outstanding human leaders in all lands call Soviet Communism?

But as to the length and the meaning of this turbulent transition period that began in 1914, how could we properly understand it from the viewpoint of the Bible prophecies as early as 1879, when these events were still over forty years ahead of us? That is why, as 1914 approached, Russell became

more convinced the transition would take longer than originally anticipated, but this in no wise changed the nature of
these startling events themselves that we knew must have a
beginning at that time.

JESUS' DISCIPLES MISTAKEN AS TO THE KINGDOM

An incident comes to mind that occurred some years after
World War II. I was giving a talk in California. One of the
old-timers who had survived the period since 1914 came to
me just before I was scheduled to go on and said, "I have a
question to ask you, Brother Mac, something that has puzzled
me for some time." I agreed to discuss it with him after the
discourse and then went on with the talk.

In the course of the talk I pointed out that a few years after
1914 we saw that what we were looking for, namely, the establishment of God's kingdom, actually did take place in 1914;
but it was a heavenly kingdom—the beginning of God's rule
earthward from the established "kingdom of the heavens."

We learned that Jesus, enthroned in heaven that year, had
immediately begun his war on Satan and his demon associates
in heaven. Satan and his demons, those rebel spirit creatures
associated with him, had been whipped and hurled to the earth,
never to return to heaven.[24] The Scriptures stated this event
was to mark the beginning of Jehovah's rule by Christ Jesus
and the beginning of a time of unparalleled trouble in the
earth.[25]

"Now," I pointed out in my talk, "had Jehovah's great war-
rior, the Lord Jesus, continued the assault against Satan and his
angels after that first skirmish which ousted those rebels from
heaven, it all would have been over before this. That had been
our view before 1914. Jehovah's war at Armageddon would
be done but, according to Jesus' statement, no flesh would
have been saved.[26] So, for the sake of God's own people, and

to fulfill his purpose, Jehovah ordered a temporary halt to the war against Satan. Jehovah 'cut short' those days of tribulation against the invisible rebel spirits by stopping his war for a period before he would resume active combat against Satan's forces at Armageddon. Furthermore, according to the prediction at Revelation 16, gathering of the kings of the whole world must occur.[27] Gathering them where? To Armageddon!—to the war of the great day of God Almighty—this to climax Jehovah's war against all wicked forces.

"So while the time of trouble for Satan and his demons began in heaven in 1914, exactly on time, and while the uninterrupted rule of earth's kings then had ended and the Lord Jesus was placed by Jehovah on the throne as king of the new world, still, as Jesus foretold in Matthew 24:14 (*New World Translation*), 'This good news of the kingdom [as being just established] will be preached in all the inhabited earth for the purpose of a witness to all the nations, and *then the accomplished end will come.*' " (Italics mine.)

My purpose in this speech at California was primarily to show why the war in heaven was halted after Satan had been cast out and how a "great multitude" was being gathered by the Lord, as foretold in the Bible book of Revelation.[28]

During the talk I made reference to the mistake Jesus' disciples had made when he was on earth. They thought he was going to break the yoke of Rome and establish his kingdom right there.[29] They were wrong as to both the time and place of his setting up his kingdom. The mistake C. T. Russell had made, I pointed out, was not as to the time, 1914, but his error was only as to *where* the kingdom had been established—in heaven instead of on earth.

After giving that talk, and while riding with that friend to the railroad station, I said: "Now what's your question, brother?"

"Well," he said, "you've already answered it."

C. T. RUSSELL'S LAST TRIP

C. T. Russell did not live long after the stirring 1914 climax to his preaching career.

In the fall of 1916 he went on a preaching tour to the West. He did not return alive. That trip proved to be his last. His final talk was in Los Angeles where he had been so weak that he had to remain seated during the talk.

As reported in the New York *Times* for November 1, 1916:

> OCTOBER 31——Charles Taze Russell, pastor of the Brooklyn Tabernacle, and known all over the country as "Pastor Russell," died from heart disease at 2:30 o'clock this afternoon on an Atchison, Topeka & Santa Fe train, en route from Los Angeles to New York. He complained of feeling ill after leaving Los Angeles, his secretary said, and gradually grew worse. The end came while the train was stopped at Pampa, Texas.

At seven o'clock the next morning (November 1) I entered Bethel dining room with a telegram just delivered. Members of the family were all seated in their customary manner and did not know anything about Russell's serious illness or death. I read them the telegram and a moan went up all over that dining room. Some wept audibly. None ate breakfast that morning. All were greatly upset.

At the end of the meal period they met in little groups to talk and whisper, "What is going to happen now?" Little work was done that day. We did not know what to do. It was so unexpected, and yet Russell had tried to prepare us for it. What *would* we do?

The first shock of our loss of C. T. Russell was the worst. For those first few days our future was a blank wall. Throughout his life Russell had been "the Society." The work centered around his dynamic determination to see God's will done. He had been a man of action. He had never had any sympathy for those merely looking to go to heaven. To him, worship of God was to expend himself in service to God, and that he had truly done. So he did not stop preaching because 1914 did not bring all that had originally been hoped for. He died as he had lived—happy in his work of preaching the Word.

We had no real organization. There had seemed no need for it. Russell had learned through many hurtsome experiences that few men could be trusted with serious responsibility. Since his prime objective was to do the harvest work, he was for getting it done before 1914 would (as he had thought until just before his death) bring an end to it. Then, as the date approached, he realized more and more that there was a far greater work to be done than the few remaining years—then months—would allow for. So with the waning of his own physical powers he had made an effort to strengthen the Society as best he could in order to keep things moving.

WHY 1914 DID NOT BRING DISAPPOINTMENT

After his funeral we returned to Bethel and began to study again. The more we studied the more determined we became to keep going in the work. One thing we knew we still had. That was something no man could take from us. It was the truth of God's Word. We had truly been "called out of darkness into God's marvelous light" and were constantly more determined to give Jehovah praise for that enlightened understanding. How much more truth we were to receive or how we were to receive it we did not know. We did not then see how anyone else could be used as Russell had been. He had written six volumes of *Studies in the Scriptures*, and we had always expected a seventh. Almost as he died Russell had said reassuringly, "Don't worry, the Lord will take care of it." We were willing to wait and see.

Our hope was real; it was a living hope. When Russell died

I was but thirty-nine. For sixteen years I had been developing a new Christian outlook. It was not something to put on or take off as suited my convenience. My faith was my very life. I did not now intend to surrender it because the future was momentarily dark. The Bible record is full of those who faced such situations, and Jehovah God always came to their rescue. We believed sincerely he would do as much for us.

We could not then have realized what we were being prepared for. But the Lord knew what he was doing in permitting these experiences to come to us, and now, forty years later, it is quite clear to us.

In those few dark years following 1914 we were experiencing the pains of travail. The New World society as it has now come to maturity was then not yet born. The dark clouds which had only begun to gather in 1916 were merely a warning of the approaching storm that was to come as close to wrecking the entire organization of Jehovah's witnesses as anything experienced before or since. The next few years truly proved to be a test of Christian fortitude and integrity.

PART **Two**

BIRTH
OF A
NATION

5

GOD'S JUDGMENT BEGINS
AT HIS HOUSE

C. T. RUSSELL WAS DEAD.
But the work for which he had given so much was not yet completed. We did not fully realize that then. Some were sure that his death would bring an end to the "harvest" work, even though he had told us plainly that there was much work yet to be done. Jesus warned the apostles frequently that he would be put to death at Jerusalem; still, when he died, they were all perplexed. We knew that Christ Jesus was Lord of the harvest, but our relationship with Russell had led us to believe that Russell himself had some special assignment that could never be filled by another. Yet Russell was dead and the work still lay open before us. We had to do something. We were perplexed for a time.

It was to our advantage that the date to elect officers for the Society was two months away. We had time to think things over, and get our minds settled, and make arrangements for the coming election. No one, at that time, wanted to take over the responsibility of control; I certainly wasn't seeking it. I felt I was just a preacher. Executive responsibility had never been my desire. We got together and formed a committee composed of J. F. Rutherford, the Society's legal counsel, who was not then an officer of the Society; W. E. Van Amburgh, who was secretary-treasurer; and A. I. Ritchie, vice-president. I was to serve as aide or assistant to this executive committee. Then we started to operate, to see what could be done to keep the work going.

At first we tried merely to hold things together, to encourage those associated with the Society to continue active and not lose their courage or their confidence. *The Watch Tower* continued to appear regularly with material that Russell had completed before his death.

As the day for election of the Society's officers approached tension began to mount. A few ambitious ones at headquarters were holding caucuses here and there, doing a little electioneering to get their men in. However, Van Amburgh and I held a large number of votes. Many shareholders, knowing of our long association with Russell, sent their proxies to us to be cast for the one whom we thought best fitted for office.

INDIVIDUALS ARE UNIMPORTANT TO GOD'S WORK

That was a grave responsibility. In order for you to appreciate the position I was in personally, perhaps I should relate an experience I had with C. T. Russell shortly before his death.

Russell always spent the forenoon from eight o'clock until twelve in his study preparing articles for *The Watch Tower* and any other writing he had to do that called for research on the Bible. Nobody went to the study in the morning unless he was sent for or had something very important, a life or death case.

About five minutes after eight one morning a stenographer said to me, "Brother Russell wants to see you in the study."

I thought, "What now?"

I walked up and knocked on the study door. He said, "Come in, brother. Please walk into the drawing room." (This was the room adjoining his study.) "I'll be with you in a moment or two."

When he walked in, with a serious expression on his face, he said, "Brother, are you as deeply interested in the truth as you were when you began?"

I looked surprised.

He continued, "Don't be surprised. That is just a leading question." Then he described his physical condition, and I knew enough about pathology to know that he would not live many more months unless he had some relief.

"Now, brother, this is what I want to talk to you about: I am no longer able to take care of the work alone. I must have someone who can be an assistant to the president. The work is increasing rapidly, and it will continue to increase, for there is a world-wide work to be done in preaching the 'gospel of the kingdom' in all the world."

He gave me a word picture of the work that I now see in progress in building up the New World society. He saw it from the Bible. I thought he was talking about something he would like to see, but to me there was not much hope that he would see it.

Then I made an unfortunate remark. "Brother Russell, what you're saying doesn't add up right in my mind."

"What do you mean, brother?"

"Your dying and this work going on. Why, when you die we all will complacently fold our arms and wait to go to heaven with you. We will quit then."

"Brother, if that is your idea, you don't see the issue. This is not man's work; it's God's work. No man is indispensable to its success. Now, you are acquainted with brothers in all parts of the country because of your extensive travel serving congregations. You can tell me who you think would be suitable for the position."

We discussed various ones from different parts of the country who were active workers preaching the kingdom message, but he did not seem to think any one of them would be suitable, or in a position to come to Brooklyn.

I moved to leave then, as it was about 11:30 A.M. There was a sliding door from the drawing room out into the hallway, and he pushed that door open. As I was going out he took hold of my arm and said, "Just a minute. You go to your room and pray to the Lord on this matter and come and tell me if Brother Macmillan will accept this position."

He closed the door and I stood there half dazed. I did think it over, very seriously, and prayed about it for some time before I finally told him I would be happy to do all that I could to assist him.

This was shortly before he went away on his final preaching tour. Before he left he wrote letters to what we then termed the heads of the different departments, outlining their duties and informing them that "A. H. Macmillan is to be in full charge of the office and the Bethel Home during my absence. Anything he says for you to do you must do; it doesn't make any difference whether you agree or not. If he tells you incorrectly, I'll attend to him when I get home." Then he handed me copies of all the letters and said, "You have the skeleton organization. Go to work and do things."

This matter weighed heavily on my mind during the two months preceding that election. Obviously Russell expected the work to go on. I had been willing to assist him in his absence, but the thought of taking full management of the entire organization appalled me. I dismissed it.

Then someone said to me, "Mac, you have a strong chance of getting in yourself. You were Brother Russell's special representative when he was gone, and he told all of us to do as you say. Well, he went away and never did return. It looks like you're the man to carry on."

"Brother," I said, "that's not the way to look at this matter. This is the Lord's work and the only position you get in the Lord's organization is what the Lord sees fit to give you; and I am sure I'm not the man for the job."

A NEW PRESIDENT TAKES OFFICE

We were still faced with the question, Who would be put up for office? Van Amburgh came to me one day and said, "Brother, who do you think we should put up for president?"

I answered, "There is only one man who is competent and qualified to take charge of this work now, and that is Brother Rutherford."

He took me by the hand and said, "I'm with you." That was all that was said about it.

Rutherford did not know what was going on. He certainly didn't do any electioneering or canvassing for votes, but I guess he was doing some worrying, knowing if he was elected he would have a big job on his hands.

On January 6, 1917, J. F. Rutherford was elected president. There is no doubt in our minds that the Lord's will was done in this choice. It is certain that Rutherford himself had nothing to do with it. W. E. Van Amburgh was elected secretary-treasurer and A. N. Pierson vice-president. Directors were not elected, as these had been elected by Russell for life. This he could do because he held the majority of votes although, according to the charter, they should have been reelected to that office every year as we learned later.

J. F. Rutherford was warmly welcomed in his new capacity as manager of the Society's affairs by the majority of those associated with the organization at that time. But from the outset it became apparent that a few, especially at headquarters, resented him. Some of these thought they should succeed Russell and considered themselves better qualified for the position of president. The fact that Rutherford was approved by the shareholders of the Society and that he made every effort to follow the arrangements made by Russell during his administration did not seem to impress them.

It is true that Rutherford was an altogether different type of man than Russell. Their backgrounds may have had something to do with it. It is certain that the home life of Russell had a definite bearing on his temperament. His father was quite well-to-do and this boy was the idol of his heart. He was brought up in the lap of luxury and in an atmosphere of parental love, although his mother died when he was quite young. Everything that he was taught he seemed to receive and respond to, and he developed a spirit of mildness and affection. There was nothing crude or rough about him in any way. He inherited that disposition and his father nourished it to the end.

As he grew older and began to associate with others in his preaching activity these characteristics became even more marked. Occasionally he had to be severe with those in the organization, but he was extremely generous, long-suffering and kind when dealing with those whom he hoped could be recovered. But with all his generosity and kindness he was by no means soft. He would never tolerate anything that would be contrary to what he clearly understood the Bible to teach. He was so strict about that, he would permit nothing that would seem to show a compromise when it came to an issue of the truth.

J. F. Rutherford's background was totally different. He was born November 8, 1869, on a farm in Morgan County, Missouri. He had no youthful life. When he was sixteen he decided to be a lawyer. In order to get his father's consent to do this he had to hire a man to fill his place on his father's farm, as well as pay tuition fees and other expenses of his education since his father would not help him. A friend gave him a loan with no security other than his word, and this money enabled him to finish his schooling. As soon as he was able he repaid the debt in full. So he received little encouragement at home. His father was a strict disciplinarian, which deprived young Rutherford of any emotional life.

When he identified himself with the work of Jehovah's witnesses and entered the ministry his pattern of life was well fixed; he already was a mature man, approaching forty, trained in the practice of law and politics. As legal counselor for the Watch Tower Society from 1907 on he developed a full knowledge of the Society's business affairs and of Russell's way of doing things.

Rutherford had always manifested a deep Christian love for his associates and was very kindhearted; but he was not naturally of the same gentle, quiet-mannered disposition as Russell. He was direct and outspoken and did not hide his feelings. His bluntness, even when spoken in kindness, was sometimes misunderstood. But he had been president only a short time when it became apparent that the Lord had chosen the right man for the job.

AN ADMINISTRATIVE CHANGE PROVIDES A TEST

To understand the current expansion of Jehovah's witnesses and the nature of their New World society it is necessary to understand the progressive development of the Society to meet the conditions that existed at each period. Russell had the necessary vision and business ability to lay a firm foundation during his administration. This was effective and accomplished Jehovah's purpose to gather together a people devoted to his Kingdom activity.

Rutherford, however, shouldered the responsibility when not only the affairs of the Society but even world conditions were in a precarious position. It was at the height of World War I, and at a time when many of those associated with the Society expected the work to end with Russell's death. Here Jehovah gave opportunity to those that were in line for His kingdom to show whether they were fully devoted to him or not, and the tests and trials that came really identified those who were more interested in themselves as individuals than they were in carrying the good news of God's kingdom to the scattered sheep.

This sifting did not come during Russell's day but it came suddenly, almost without warning, during the first two years of Rutherford's administration.

Russell had been president of the Society from the time it was incorporated until he died, in 1916, and some looked up to him with what almost amounted to creature worship. His mature understanding of the Scriptures and his ability to expound them was so far beyond that of any other person that very few would criticize or find fault with him or his explanations of the Bible. However, Rutherford was not only an entirely different type of man, but he had come into association with our movement later than some of those who opposed him. So when he became president it began to appear that some were associated with us not because of the love of the truth or the desire to be in the service of Jehovah, so much as for the personal enjoyment of fellowship with a man like Russell. But when Rutherford came in he was all for advancing the work. His attitude was, "Let's get the work done. Don't come around palavering over me." To some this was a severe test. They had so admired the natural qualities of Russell that they thought they must and could develop the same qualities. Some became so full of that idea they could not see the strength and integrity of a man like Rutherford, nor could they reconcile these attributes with the love that he kept on trying to manifest toward all. So to some it became a matter of personalities altogether; and the question we all were forced to decide was, Are we in the organization just to associate with a man who has a pleasing disposition and who brings comfort and joy, or are we in here because we love Jehovah and want to share unitedly with him and Christ Jesus in doing his work?

It was a time of trying experiences, of great pressures within and without the organization, and Rutherford himself learned much about dealing with his associates as well as establishing the preaching organization of Jehovah's witnesses.

PERSONAL AMBITION DISRUPTS THE WORK

Russell gave me definite instructions before leaving on his last preaching tour. He suggested certain changes in the office force: some were to be assigned to different work. I at once made these changes. However, after Russell's death I was criticized for doing so.

Another instruction Russell gave me before leaving was to arrange to send one of our traveling representatives, P. S. L. Johnson, to England. He should try to preach the good news to the troops wherever possible. Talking to the soldiers about the Kingdom of God would comfort them as they prepared for action.

The executive committee, of which Rutherford was chairman, arranged to send Johnson to England according to Russell's wish as expressed to me. In addition to preaching to the troops, he was to make a tour of England and visit the congregations scattered all over that land, and comfort them in their war-time anxiety, encouraging them to continue steadfast in the work of preaching the Kingdom of God as the hope of mankind. In general he was to learn all he could about the progress of the work in England. He was to make a full report on conditions there and offer suggestions as to how things might be improved. This report was to be made to the

Society, but Johnson was not to make any changes in the personnel at the British headquarters. If anything of that kind seemed necessary, the Society would consider it on the basis of his report.

When Johnson arrived in England in November, 1916, he was given a warm and hearty welcome by the friends. They were having many problems to solve after the death of Russell, and were glad to have a representative from headquarters with them. Johnson was welcomed everywhere he went. He could tell them many things about Russell's death, and the progress the work was making in America.

The attention heaped upon him began to warp his judgment and finally his reason, until he came to the ridiculous conclusion that he was the "steward" of Jesus' parable of the penny.[1] He later thought he was the world's high priest. His conduct in England caused much confusion and deep concern about the work there. He tried to seize control of the Society's bank account in London and summarily dismissed some of the London headquarters' staff with no authority to do so. Rutherford, who in the meantime was elected president of the Society, saw that he must act promptly to save the work in England from disruption.

He cabled Johnson, canceling his appointment and recalling him to the United States. After many cables were sent by Johnson trying to show that he was much needed in England and that he should be given control of the British field, he finally heeded Rutherford's recall. After his return to America he tried to persuade Rutherford to return him to England to complete his work there, but was unsuccessful. His failure to get back to England led him to think that Rutherford was not the right man to be president of the Society. He, Johnson, was the man with the ability necessary to be president.

The next step was to influence the board of directors to compel Rutherford to send him back to England. Seemingly he had little trouble gaining the support of four of them. He persuaded them to oppose the president in an effort to run the Society in their own way. They concluded that they were going to take a hand in the Johnson matter and show their authority. "It isn't good for Rutherford to control the management of the Society's affairs. We'll inform him that he can be the president; that is, he'll just be a figurehead. He will go out on the road under our direction to lecture but, as a board of directors, we will manage the Society, direct its policies and look after all its affairs. Van Amburgh will be our secretary-treasurer and we will have the whole thing in our own hands." This was in the spring of 1917. Rutherford knew that Johnson was counseling them in this matter, still he was extremely patient throughout the entire ordeal. In view of what Johnson had done to show his lack of real concern for the Society's welfare, Rutherford had every reason to dismiss him from the Bethel home. But he didn't. Neither did he take action to interfere with the rebellious plot being hatched to oppose him in his office as president. He did everything that he could to help his opposers see their mistake, holding a number of meetings with them, trying to reason with them and show them how contrary their course was to the Society's charter and to the entire program Russell had followed since the organization was formed. He even came to several of us and asked, "Shall I resign as president and let those opposing ones take charge?" We all replied, "Brother, the Lord put you where you are, and to resign or quit would be disloyalty to the Lord." Furthermore, the office force threatened they would quit if these men got control.

Matters began to come to a head when, at an extended session of the 1917 annual meeting, these four directors endeavored to present a resolution to amend the by-laws of the Society to place administrative powers in the hands of the Board of Directors. This was not only contrary to the organizational arrangement practiced by Russell for the entire thirty-two years of his administration, but it was contrary to the

expressed wish of the shareholders. Rutherford was forced to
rule the motion out of order, and from then on the opposition
grew stiffer and more determined.

REBELLIOUS ACTION FORCES A SHOWDOWN

Faced with the certainty that these men would try to tie up
the funds of the Society by court action (as Johnson had attempted in London), Rutherford decided he would have to
act. The time for strategic action in the interest of all concerned had come.

He was preparing to go on a preaching trip to the West
and was much concerned about what his opposers might do
while he was gone. He said to me: "Brother, these men may
try to start something while I'm away, but don't be fearful
or worried about what they might try to do."

"If they try to take hold of things while you are gone what
shall I do?" I asked.

"If they get too obstreperous and indicate they want to
start action against the Society, call a policeman."

"What! A policeman?"

"Yes, if it becomes necessary, don't hesitate."

But I did not understand the operation of his legal mind.
Well, sure enough, one day while Rutherford was away, I
was in the office down on Hicks Street with our office manager, Robert J. Martin. These four dignitaries who thought
they were directors marched down to Van Amburgh's desk
in the rear of the office and said, "Brother Van Amburgh, we
order you upstairs to the chapel." That was on the second
floor right over the office. "We want you up there to transact some business."

Van Amburgh knew what was coming and said, "Don't
bother me, friends. Go about your business; I have my work
to do."

"We want you up there. We need to have a quorum." There were four of them, which was a majority of the board. There were seven on the board, and to transact legal business a quorum of five was necessary. I was watching what was going on. The other workers were all looking on nervously and worrying about what was going to take place.

The four went upstairs and sat down and began talking about what they would do. I was worried too. I knew that if they could obtain a quorum to transact business they could railroad new bylaws through that would change the complete structure of the organization. I waited a little while and said, "Brother Martin, let's go up and see what those brothers are doing." When we got up there they ordered me out.

"We've had enough of you. You've been trying to run this place because Pastor Russell left you in charge of the work, but now we are in charge! You get out of here."

At that time I was vice-president of our New York corporation. Therefore in the absence of President Rutherford, I had control and responsibility for the property owned by the Society. I did not remind them of this point but told Martin to call a policeman.

He found an old Irishman, a typical old fellow, who came in twirling a long night stick around in his hand. He said, "Well, gentlemen, what's the trouble here?"

I said, "Officer, these men have no business here. Their place is up at 124 Columbia Heights, and they are disturbing our work here. They refused to leave when we ordered them to. Now we just thought we would call upon the law."

They jumped up and began to argue. The policeman twirled his stick around and said:

"Gentlemen, it's after being serious for you now. Faith, and I know these two, Macmillan and Martin, but you fellows I don't know. Now you better be after going, for fear there'll be trouble."

They grabbed their hats and went down the steps two at a
time, and hurried up to Borough Hall to get in touch with a
lawyer. They were fighting mad. Rutherford told me afterward that is the very reason he had told me to bring the
policeman in, to draw their fire. They had been sneaking
around in an underhanded way trying to disturb the congregations and interfere with the work. He knew that, and calling the policeman brought the issue to a head. Now the matter must be settled in some way in order to restore unity to
the organization.

Although thoroughly familiar with the legal organization
of the Society, he took the matter to a prominent corporation
lawyer in Philadelphia to determine the status of the board
of directors. Through a written opinion he received, he discovered that these four men were not legally members of the
board at all! Russell had elected them as directors for life but
the law stipulated that directors must be elected by the vote
of the shareholders each year. However, Rutherford, Pierson
and Van Amburgh were directors because they had been
elected to the office of president, vice-president and secretary-treasurer. The fact that they were elected as officials
made them members of the board. Since the four opposers
were not legally elected they had no legal authority to act
for the Society; and since the attitude they had displayed
showed they were not qualified, it was a simple procedure for
Rutherford to appoint other directors for the existing vacan-
cies until the next legal election.

The climax came in July of 1917, only six months after
Rutherford had been elected president. He had arranged to
produce the seventh volume of *Studies in the Scriptures*. Rus-
sell had written the first six. The seventh, called *The Finished
Mystery*, was really a compilation of material from notes and
writings of Russell and was issued as a posthumous work of
Russell's. Since, according to the bylaws, the president of the
Society was also manager of the Society's affairs, Rutherford

had not consulted the board of directors and the four who thought they were members raised vehement objections. As a result, their opposition to the policy and work of the Society became so bitter that it was impossible to maintain unity at headquarters as long as they remained. They were asked to leave the Bethel home or get in line with the work. They chose to leave.

However, it was not Rutherford's wish to ignore them altogether. He gave them every opportunity to manifest a spirit of cooperation and even offered them the position of traveling representatives of the Society, but they refused. Finally, they completely withdrew themselves from association with the Society and started an organization of their own.

SPIRITUAL FOOD FOR THOSE APPROVED

You may wonder why I'm telling you all of these things, why I should be willing to "air our family troubles," so to speak. It certainly was one of the most painful experiences I ever went through in my entire life, to see those who had once manifested a zeal for the Lord's work, with whom we had been closely associated for a number of years, now, because they did not receive the honor they thought was due them, try to get control of the Lord's organization. But that is why it becomes such an important part of my story. Not only are these events a matter of actual record, but they form a significant part of the evidences in fulfillment of Bible prophecy. This was a weeding out, a time of judgment, a cleansing of the entire organization set apart to become the household of God's servants.[2]

All of those associated were forced to make a decision. Would they continue with the organization which Jehovah had been using up to that time and which he had obviously blessed, or would they follow some individuals more interested in personal opinions than in carrying on the harvest work? Some left the organization with their disgruntled leaders; although the majority did not hesitate to show their appreciation for the course Rutherford had taken and to manifest their confidence in his determination to see the Lord's will done.

All of us were inclined to wonder and to exclaim, "How strange that we should have such trials now!" Then we were reminded of the words of the apostle Peter: [3] "Beloved, do not be surprised at the fiery ordeal which comes upon you to prove you, as though something strange were happening to you."

True, Jesus had said: [4] "By this all men will know that you are my disciples, if you have love for one another." But on the very day he uttered these words he was betrayed by one of those professing love for him! It is not strange, then, that some within the modern congregation would follow the same kind of course, disrupting the family peace and threatening the life of the organization itself. In fact, one of the four opposers said they would rather see the Society wrecked than have Rutherford control it.

Such a division was inevitable in view of the prophecy Jesus gave of how he would clean out all of those not truly interested in feeding his flock. He promised to return and seat his servants at a table to eat food that he himself would serve.[5] But, he pointed out, some of the watchers would not be faithfully performing their duties; in fact, they would be beating and abusing their fellow-servants. These, he said, he would gather out and cast aside.[6]

The important work which lay ahead, for which the Lord was preparing his people, would require a unified organization composed of only those who were willing, obedient and faithful.

The prophet Malachi foretold a necessary cleansing before

this great work of giving the witness to the whole world would be undertaken. Said he: [7] "The messenger of the covenant, whom ye desire, behold, he cometh, saith Jehovah . . . and he will purify the sons of Levi, and refine them as gold and silver; and they shall offer unto Jehovah offerings in righteousness." These would be fed at the table of Jehovah in order to receive strength to carry out their responsible assignment.

The internal struggle which was now successfully weathered had taken its toll. But our worst encounter was yet to come.

CHAPTER 6

"MISCHIEF FRAMED BY LAW"

THE FIRST SEVERE SHOCK of internal dissension had failed to disrupt the organization. Those of us who held fast were drawn even closer together in our determination to uphold Scriptural principles and press on in the harvest work which some of us still were thinking might be drawing to a close. But our preaching activity was much like the "sackcloth" condition described in the book of Revelation.[1]

External opposition had been mounting for some time. Especially the leaders of most of the religious organizations were bitter in their denunciation of our activity. They resented our calling attention to the evidences that pointed to 1914 as the beginning of the end, and especially the awkward position in which it placed them due to their own active participation in world affairs of the time. William Jennings Bryan, as Secretary of State to President Woodrow Wilson, had made a tour of the country urging the United States of America to stay out of World War I, while most of the clergy were urging the government to get into it. Bryan resigned when, April 6, 1917, the United States entered the war.

February 12, 1918, a number of the Society's publications, including the book, *The Finished Mystery*, were banned in Canada. The public press there recognized and openly mentioned the prominent part the clergy played in this action. The Winnipeg *Tribune* at that time said: "The banned publications are alleged to contain seditious and antiwar statements. Excerpts from one of the recent issues of the *Bible Students Monthly* [2] were denounced from the pulpit a few weeks ago by Rev. Charles G. Patterson, Pastor of St. Stephen's Church. Afterward Attorney General Johnson sent to Rev. Patterson for a copy of the publication. The censor's order is believed to be the direct result."

The day following this order in Canada prohibiting circulation of *The Finished Mystery* United States Government agents of the department of secret service seized the books of the Watch Tower Bible and Tract Society at 17 Hicks Street, Brooklyn. Nothing detrimental was found. Then, February 24, 1918, Rutherford delivered for the first time a lecture that has since become world famous. The startling subject was "The World Has Ended—Millions Now Living May Never Die." This was delivered at Clune's Auditorium in Los Angeles, California. In developing his evidences that the world really did end in 1914, Rutherford pointed, among other things, to the world war then raging, as part of the "sign," foretold by Jesus. He then fixed much of the responsibility for these conditions on the world's religious leaders. He admitted there were good clergymen as well as bad, just as there are good and bad lawyers, but he pointed out:

As a class, according to the Scriptures, the clergymen are the most reprehensible men on earth for the great war that is now afflicting mankind. For 1,500 years they have taught the people the satanic doctrine of the divine right of kings to rule. They have mixed politics and religion, church and state; have proved disloyal to their God-given privilege of proclaiming the message of Messiah's kingdom, and have given themselves over to encouraging the rulers to believe that the king reigns by divine right, and therefore whatsoever he does is right. So thoroughly has this been impressed upon men that the great law writer, Blackstone, incorporated in his commentaries: "The king can do no wrong."

The following day (February 25, 1918) a full-page report of the lecture was printed in the Los Angeles *Morning Tribune*. Prominent clergymen were so angered by this report that the ministerial association held a meeting that same day and sent its president to the manager of the paper, demanding an explanation as to why they had published so much about the lecture. It was only three days later that the United States Army Intelligence Bureau at Los Angeles took possession of our Los Angeles headquarters, confiscating many of the Society's publications. Now began a period of constant harassment by members of the Intelligence Bureau in an effort to dig up something that could be used in evidence against us on a charge of violating the Espionage Law.

A CONSPIRACY COMES TO LIGHT

On June 15, 1917, Congress had provided for conscripting manpower by passing the Selective Draft Act, which also provided that men who had conscientious scruples against engaging in war because of religious belief might be exempted from combatant service. Many young men wrote the Watch Tower Society and asked Judge Rutherford what course they should take. He refused to give advice as to what they should do, but stated, in effect, "If you cannot conscientiously engage in war, Section 3 of the Selective Draft Act makes provision for you to file application for exemption. You should register and file your application for exemption, setting forth

the reason, and the draft board will pass on your application."
He never did more than to advise them to take advantage of
the Act of Congress.

Great pressure was put on him to do more. A number of
young men of draft age associated with the Watch Tower
Bible and Tract Society had been sent as conscientious objectors to Camp Upton, Long Island, New York. This army
camp was under the direction of General James Franklin
Bell.[3]

Bell made a personal visit to the office of J. F. Rutherford
and tried to persuade him to write a letter instructing these
young men to take whatever service he might assign them,
even if it were across the sea. Rutherford refused, pointing
out it was a matter for everyone to decide for himself. His
reply angered General Bell.

Later Rutherford, accompanied by Van Amburgh, visited
General Bell at Camp Upton. There General Bell, in the
presence of his aide and the two officers of the Watch Tower
Society, made a startling admission, as Rutherford reported
years later [4] in a published statement. Bell told about a conference of a large number of clergymen in Philadelphia in
1917. These men had appointed a committee to visit Washington, D. C., to insist on a revision of the Selective Draft
Act and the Espionage Law. They selected John Lord O'Brian
of the Department of Justice to introduce a bill to have all
cases against the Espionage Law tried before a military court
with the death penalty imposed as punishment. Bell stated
with considerable feeling: "That bill did not pass, because
Wilson prevented it; but we know how to get you, and *we
are going to do it!*"

ACCUSED OF OPPOSING THE DRAFT

In the meantime, at the request of the Attorney General,
Congress was undertaking to amend the Espionage Law to

make it more effective against the dissemination of propaganda. However, a provision called the France Amendment was introduced to exempt from the provisions of the Espionage Act any individual who uttered "what is true, with good motives and for justifiable ends." This amendment was adopted by the Senate after a long debate in order to exclude from punishment as seditionists those who indulge in what the Senators called honest criticism. Later, at the instance of the Department of Justice, the House and Senate conferees on other amendments for the Espionage Act eliminated the France Amendment, recommending to Congress that the Espionage Act be amended without it. When the conferees' report was presented to the Senate, it was argued that inclusion of the France Amendment would make convictions extremely difficult; and a letter was read into the *Congressional Record* from John Lord O'Brian, Special Assistant Attorney General, strongly opposing it. He said: [5]

> The Espionage Act has proved a fairly effective weapon against propaganda, and if amended as requested by the department by making attempts to obstruct enlistment impossible, there is every reason to believe that it will be thoroughly effective. Its effectiveness for the purpose of killing propaganda, however, has come from the principle that motives prompting propaganda are irrelevant. . . . For example, the most dangerous type of propaganda used in this country is religious pacifism: i.e., opposition to the war on the ground that it is opposed to the Word of God. This is a type of propaganda which was extensively used in weakening the Italian armies. The statements used in it generally consist of quotations from the Bible and various interpretations thereof. Convictions against this type of propaganda are only possible where the motive is irrelevant and our juries can be made to *infer the intent* from the natural effect of a propaganda.

On May 4 another letter from O'Brian was read into the *Record* to buttress the Justice Department's position, and in it he cited and commended the position taken on this point of intent by a United States District Judge of Vermont, Harland B. Howe.[6] (We of the Watch Tower Society were unaware of Howe's views until after he had been chosen to preside, later, at our own trial.) That our Society then already was definitely marked for prosecution is clear according to another memorandum submitted at the same time by the Attorney General and also placed in the *Congressional Record*. Speaking of printed matter which, in the opinion of the Intelligence Service, "could only serve to stir men up to mutiny and tend to disintegrate our entire army," the memorandum stated: [7]

> One of the most dangerous examples of this sort of propaganda is the book called *The Finished Mystery*, a work written in extremely religious language and distributed in enormous numbers. The only effect of it is to lead the soldiers to discredit our cause and to inspire a feeling at home of resistance to the draft. The Kingdom News,[8] of Brooklyn, prints a petition demanding that restrictions on *The Finished Mystery* and similar works should be removed, "so that people may be permitted, without interference or molestation, to buy, sell, have, and read this aid to Bible study." The passage of this amendment would reopen our camps to this poisonous influence.
>
> The International Bible Students' Association [9] pretends to the most religious motives, yet we have found that its headquarters have long been reported as the resort of German agents.

As a result of this intense campaign of the Department of Justice, on May 4, 1918, the Senate approved the Conferees' Report, and the amended Espionage Act was approved, without the France Amendment, May 16, 1918. Ten days earlier (May 7) the Department of Justice had obtained warrants from the United States District Court for the Eastern District of New York authorizing the arrest of the Watch Tower

Bible and Tract Society's officers. These included J. F. Rutherford, W. E. Van Amburgh, F. H. Robison, R. J. Martin,
C. J. Woodworth, George H. Fisher, Giovanni De Cecca
and myself.

The next day, May 8, the Department's agents pounced
upon us, arresting those of us who were at Bethel. Eventually
all eight of us were taken into custody.

Bail was set at $2,500 each, and we were released until the
day set for trial, June 3, 1918, in the United States District
Court for the Eastern District of New York.

That was a painful experience for us and brings to mind
the Scripture at Psalm 94:20, 21 (*Revised Standard Version*),
"Can wicked rulers be allied with thee, who frame mischief
by statute? They band together against the life of the righteous, and condemn the innocent to death."

Temporarily free on bond, we continued our work comforted with the thought expressed in Verse Twenty-two of
this Psalm: "But the Lord has become my stronghold, and
my God the rock of my refuge."

CHAPTER 7

SENTENCED TO EIGHTY YEARS
FOR PREACHING THE GOSPEL

ONE DAY just before our trial was due to begin a group of men came into Bethel and asked to see J. F. Rutherford. Since he was busy at the time I asked them: "Gentlemen, what do you desire?"

"Well," the spokesman said, "we represent an organization that is interested in civil liberties and we want to know something about this prosecution. We read in the paper about your arrest."

"As far as we know, gentlemen, it is just the anger of one powerful religious organization working against us because we have exposed some of their false teachings."

"Don't fool yourself, sir, it isn't just one organization that is active against you. There is a definite campaign on to stop your work."

"How do you know that?"

"We are interested in such things and this kind of activity

is rampant just now. There are a large number of minority groups that are not popular and those in certain places of authority are pouncing on them, trying to wipe them out, and that is what they are going to do to you if they can."

That is what proved to be the case.

TRIED FOR CONSPIRACY

The trial opened June 3, 1918. Because of the feeling that had been manifested in our preliminary hearings we filed affidavits showing why we believed Judge Garvin was biased against us. This automatically transferred the case to Judge Chatfield, but since there was no qualified judge without bias and prejudice who wanted to try the case, United States District Judge Harland B. Howe was brought in from Vermont to preside. This was the same Judge Howe mentioned by O'Brian in the letter I referred to earlier. So, while it was known to the Government that Howe had special prejudice in favor of the prosecution of the law and against the defendants charged with violating it, it was not known to us. But we were not left long in the dark. From the first conference of the attorneys in the judge's chambers before the trial began his animosity was manifested, and he indicated, "I'm going to give these defendants all that is coming to them." However, it was now too late for our attorneys to file an affidavit of prejudice on the part of the judge.

Our indictment was in four counts, each count charging a separate and distinct offense under different parts of the statute. This statute, known as the Espionage Law, was enacted June 15, 1917, and was strictly a war measure. It would be impossible to violate it when the country is at peace.

The indictment as originally returned charged that a conspiracy was entered into some time between April 6, 1917, the date the United States declared war, and the sixth day of

May, 1918. Upon motion the Government specified the date of the alleged offense as between June 15, 1917, and May 6, 1918.

A conspiracy is an agreement between two or more persons to commit an unlawful act. At the trial the Government contended that *The Finished Mystery* was written and published designedly to hinder the United States in raising an army and prosecuting the war and that the defendants had written letters to members of the Society within draft age that interfered with the raising of an army. *The Finished Mystery* was offered in evidence by the Government and portions of it read, particularly the preface, pages 247–252, 406, 407 and 469. The Government counsel contended that these pages were designedly hidden in different parts of the book for the purpose of getting a person interested in some other part of the book and then influencing him by the statements concerning war; that publishing the book, *The Bible Students Monthly* and *The Watch Tower*, as well as writing letters to conscientious objectors, all were overt acts in carrying out the conspiracy.

On June 10 Mr. Oeland, Special Assistant Attorney General, as prosecutor for the Government, said: [1] "The Government rests, if your Honor please, except for some motions."

Judge Howe asked: "Now, have you introduced some evidence tending to show some act of each of the defendants here in furtherance of this alleged conspiracy?"

"Yes, sir."

"As to Rutherford and Van Amburgh, I am clear about, and the two defendants who wrote the seventh volume I am clear about them, Woodworth and Fisher. Now, as to the defendant De Cecca, who was the one who wrote these letters, I am clear about him, and Martin, who was the manager, I am clear about him, and Robison. That leaves Mr. Macmillan."

"As to Mr. Macmillan," Oeland replied, "there is a check

in evidence which the witness, Mr. Conkey, said was in payment of the books, of these books, [that check being] countersigned by Mr. Macmillan; then the additional fact testified to
by the first woman witness, Mrs. Campbell, that Macmillan
was the general manager in the absence of Mr. Rutherford,
attending to the correspondence in Mr. Rutherford's absence.
As I recall it, she testified that Macmillan was the general manager and he was Mr. Rutherford's assistant, that is what she
said, and acted whenever he was absent. Some testimony was
given by that same witness, Mr. Hudgings, that in Rutherford's absence he took—he ran the whole place in Rutherford's
absence."

"You have not shown any act or acts of Macmillan except
his signing of the checks."

"That is the only act outside of the fact that I asked this
lady and she said in Mr. Rutherford's absence he gave her
directions as to what to do in the office and I asked the same
fact of Mr. Hudgings. I think I asked her if she had general
directions in Mr. Rutherford's absence——"

Mr. Fuller, one of our attorneys, interrupted: "I think the
testimony is that she understood that he looked after matters
in Mr. Rutherford's absence; in respect to the correspondence
she said she couldn't say, testified that he sort of helped out.
In other words, that she understood he was in a representative
capacity, but could not specify with any degree of particular-
ity what character of duties he performed."

Judge Howe then said: "If there is no evidence tending to
show he conspired, he will be discharged."

It was then established that the check was turned over in
payment on a general open running account for printed literature. Actually, it became apparent that the Government expected to convict me of conspiracy simply on the fact that I
had countersigned a check used in part for payment in printing the questionable book, which according to the evidence

submitted I might never even have seen before it was published. Then Judge Howe said, "Well, the Government rests. What will the defendants do first?"

THE PROSECUTION MAKES ANOTHER ATTEMPT

Immediately our attorneys submitted motions for dismissal in our behalf on the ground that no cause of action had been proved. The Government had admitted that the book was written before the United States entered the war and before the Selective Draft Act and Espionage Law had been passed, so no intent to interfere with these laws could be shown in the writing of the book. The effort was then made to show that after the laws had been passed by Congress continued sale of the seventh volume constituted intent and established conspiracy.

Judge Howe denied all of the motions to dismiss us except that in my favor, and he reserved decision on that until the next day.

Some of our people who were attending the trial later told me that one of the attorneys for the Government had gone out into the hallway, where he talked in low tones to some of those who had led the opposition within the Society. They said, "Don't let that fellow go; he's the worst of the bunch. He'll keep things going if you don't get him with the others."

That night the eight of us gathered in our attorneys' office to discuss the evidence that had been put in and decided on what points should be brought out when court reconvened. Finally one of our attorneys turned to me, saying, "Do you know that tomorrow morning we can have you released? Do you want to go to prison if you are convicted?"

I said: "Mr. Fuller, if these men, my friends, are going to

the Atlanta prison or any other place for preaching the gospel, I want to go with them."

"Do you mean that? That might mean something serious to you."

"I mean every word of it."

He smiled, and said, "Now if you are convicted and you remain there, it will help our case on appeal."

The next morning the Government reopened its case and introduced a paper which they testified had been taken from the Society's offices. They read parts of it to the jury and said it was a record of a meeting of the board of directors during which publication of *The Finished Mystery* was discussed. The prosecution indicated it was signed by all of the Society's officers including me. They said that the seventh volume was the issue in prosecuting us, and if I had endorsed the publication, then I was in the conspiracy.

This is what the record indicated as to my part in the publication of the book. The quotation is from a signed statement of facts read by Rutherford to the board to acquaint them with his activities since he had become president about seven months previous. Among other things it said: "It seemed good to the Lord to have the seventh volume prepared, and two faithful brethren, Brothers Woodworth and Fisher, did this work, other faithful ones assisting in the mechanical part of it. I have read considerable of the manuscript and printers' proof while traveling on trains. When the time came for publishing this work we were in the midst of much opposition [from the four of our associates who believed themselves directors] and, knowing that to consult the opposers would hinder the publishing of the volume, I took counsel with Brothers Van Amburgh, Macmillan, Martin and Hudgings, of the office force. After praying over the matter the Lord seemed to open the way so that the opposition might not interfere. A certain brother, without solicitation, placed in my hands the necessary money with which this book should be published, and the

Lord's favor seeming to be upon it the publication was under-taken."

Then the question came up as to my signature on this paper. Nobody could identify it. The prosecution called to the stand William F. Hudgings, who had charge of all the Society's printing. They put him on the stand, and because he insisted he could not identify my signature Judge Howe finally ad-judged him guilty of contempt of court and ordered him com-mitted to jail—even though he was the Government's witness. On the same day the grand jury indicted him for perjury. Pleading not guilty, he obtained an order for release on bail but was unable to avail himself of it because he continued to be held under the commitment for contempt. In fact, the com-mitment directed that it should continue in force until the witness had purged himself of the contempt for which he was being punished. It was not until a writ of habeas corpus was allowed by the Supreme Court of the United States and a de-cision rendered in his favor that he was released on bail De-cember 12, 1918. Finally, April 14, 1919, ten months after his commitment, the Supreme Court decision in his favor was an-nounced. In writing the opinion of the Supreme Court,[2] Chief Justice White stated that the lower court "had exceeded its jurisdiction by punishing as a contempt an act which it had no power to so punish, and that even if the act punished was sus-ceptible of being treated as a contempt the action of the court was arbitrary, beyond the limits of any discretion possessed, and violative of due process of law under the Fifth Amend-ment." This "arbitrary" attitude of Judge Howe, identified expressly in the *Hudgings* opinion by the Chief Justice of the United States, well represented Howe's attitude throughout the trial.

After Hudgings failed to identify my signature a former officer of the Society was sworn in and he said he could iden-tify the signature. He couldn't remember ever having seen me write anything but he said, "That is his signature."

OUR DEFENSE SHOWS NO INTENT

After the Government had completed its case we presented our defense. In essence we showed that the Society is wholly a religious organization; that the members accept as their principles of belief the holy Bible as expounded by Charles T. Russell; that C. T. Russell in his lifetime wrote and published six volumes, *Studies in the Scriptures*, and as early as 1896 promised the seventh volume which would treat Ezekiel and Revelation; that on his death bed he stated that someone else would write the seventh volume; that shortly after his death the executive committee of the Society authorized C. J. Woodworth and George H. Fisher to write and submit manuscript for consideration without any promise made concerning publication; that the manuscript on Revelation was completed before the United States got into the war and all the manuscript of the entire book (except a chapter on the Temple) was in the hands of the printer before the enactment of the Espionage Law; hence, it was impossible for any such conspiracy as charged to have been entered into to violate the law.

We testified that we never at any time combined, agreed or conspired to do anything whatsoever to affect the draft or interfere with the Government in the prosecution of the war, nor did we have any thought of so doing; that we never had any intention of interfering in any manner with the war; that our work was wholly religious and not at all political; that we did not solicit members and never advised or encouraged anyone to resist the draft; that the letters written were to those whom we knew to be dedicated Christians who were entitled under the law to advice; that we were not opposed to the nation going to war, but as dedicated Christians could not engage in mortal combat.

At the trial it was apparent to us that the prosecution, with consent of Judge Howe (and also in his charge to the jury), aimed for conviction, insisting our motive was irrelevant and that intent should be inferred from our acts. The Attorney General had designed the Espionage Law to make such prosecutions possible even though having "a clear idea of the results which would follow from the enforcement of this statute." Later O'Brian himself admitted this, reporting that all United States Attorneys had been immediately warned "against dangers of abuse under this law." Publicity given the law "fanned animosities into flame, vastly increasing the amount of suspicion and complaints throughout the country." Even influential Felix Frankfurter wrote Secretary of War Baker that "conscientious objectors . . . be turned over to the Fort Leavenworth authorities for treatment."[3] We were caught in a tide of popular opinion.

The case went to the jury June 20 about 5 P.M., and at 9:40 P.M. the same night they came in with their verdict. The Clerk of Court said, "Have you reached a verdict, gentlemen?"

"Yes. Guilty on all four counts."

"Is Defendant Macmillan found guilty also?"

"Yes."

Next day at high noon Judge Howe pronounced sentence.

COMMITTED TO THE PENITENTIARY

We all were present; the courtroom was packed. When asked by the court if we had anything to say none of us responded.

Judge Howe in sentencing us said, in a spirit of anger: "The religious propaganda in which these men are engaged is more harmful than a division of German soldiers [1,200 men]. They have not only called in question the law officers of the Government and the army intelligence bureau but have *denounced all the ministers of all the churches*. Their punishment should be severe." [4] (Italics mine.)

We remarked at the time as to the similarity of these words with those used against Stephen, the first Christian martyr.[5]

The religious leaders stirred up the people against Stephen because they were unable to resist the wisdom and spirit by which he spoke. They charged that "this man ceaseth not to speak blasphemous words against this holy place [the Jewish ecclesiastical system], and against the law."

We were sentenced to eighty years in the penitentiary. Sentence for Giovanni De Cecca was delayed for further information. He finally received forty years. All sentences were on four counts, to run concurrently; which meant that seven of us could look forward to twenty years in Atlanta.

We were kept in Brooklyn's Raymond Street jail. It was the dirtiest hole I ever got into. C. J. Woodworth, one of our group sentenced, said there were four kinds of bedbugs there; and I asked him how he knew. "Why," he said, "I have four kinds of lumps on my body."

We navigated along there for a week. Then we were sent for another week down to Long Island City prison. Finally on the fourth of July we were bundled up and sent to Atlanta by train.

From the tone of some of the newspaper accounts, there was considerable rejoicing in certain quarters over our conviction. It was obvious that the clergymen of some religions thought they had the Watch Tower Society killed and out of the way for all time. Circumstances that developed certainly seemed to indicate that. It made me think of John the Baptist when Herod had him beheaded, and of how John's disciples came and took the body and buried it. In other words, after being killed, John was put back to the dust he came from. The Society was organized and incorporated in Allegheny, Pennsylvania. Well, those left in charge at Brooklyn were forced by circumstances to take the Society's headquarters right back where it came from and bury it there--in a bit of a building on Federal Street.

Judge Howe and, later, Circuit Judge Martin Manton both

denied bail pending appeal of our case, so we were hurried away to Atlanta before a third application for bail was heard at Washington by Justice Brandeis of the Supreme Court of the United States. Getting into a new home with prospects of being there twenty years was a trying experience.

THE DEPUTY WARDEN BECOMES DISTURBED

At first we were put in the tailor shop making buttonholes and sewing buttons on prisoners' clothes. They put Rutherford to making those little jackets the prisoners wear. There was no collar on them, just sleeves and pockets. Giovanni De Cecca, who is still a member of our headquarters staff, relates how Rutherford worked on one for a long time and even then he did not finish it. One of the guards, Giovanni said, was just a little fellow but he "trimmed the judge down," and Rutherford was a big man, six feet, four. But the guard was so unreasonable that some of the other prisoners, three or four Italians and some Jews, out of pity for him, took hold of the jacket and finished it in just a few minutes. For that consideration and kindness shown by these other prisoners who never had seen him before, Rutherford actually had tears in his eyes. Eventually Rutherford was transferred to the library, where he was much more at home with the work.

At first most of the prisoners and guards were against us, because they had been given a false impression. But gradually their attitude changed. Then, when Christmas time came, our friends outside sent us so many things that we could not use all of them ourselves. Rutherford asked permission from the warden to pass some around to prisoners who had not received anything from home. He readily granted permission, and even provided paper bags for our use. We were able to give out about fifteen hundred packages of stuff.

Of course I got into some trouble there, as I do almost every place I go; but it was not really serious. One of the trusties approached me and offered to sell me a little trunk, a sort of box to keep things in my cell. He said, "Put a lock on it, put your personal things in it and when a trusty comes in to clean up your cell during the day he can't get into it."

"Well, what do you want for it?" I had no money, of course, but finally we settled for a safety razor and I put the box in my cell. Where did he get it, do you suppose? Later I found out that trusty had stolen it from the officers' mess. It was a bread box they had made to keep bread in so it would not get stale.

The guards started searching the whole plant from one end to another. They even looked in the stall of old Bill, the mule, to see if it was in there. Then they found it in my cell. The Deputy Warden called me down to his office. He was judge, jury and executioner for any crime inside the penitentiary. The dungeon was right back of his office, in through a narrow door, and there you were put if found guilty. We called it "the hole." Of course, the prisoners knew about this "frisking" that had been going on. By this time all the prisoners had become acquainted with us and when they saw me going down to the Deputy's office they said, "Oh Mac is in, he'll be in the hole for six months."

When I entered the Deputy's office he said, "Well, you know what I called you for. You were found with contraband in your cell."

"Yes, I got a box in there."

"Where did you get it?"

"From Murphy."

"What did you give him for it?"

"A safety razor."

"Do you know where he got it?"

"No, I haven't the slightest idea."

"Why, he stole it from the officers' mess."

"Well, I didn't know that."

"Well, we'll forget it. I know you didn't. But I want to talk to you. What do you think of this place you are in anyway?"

I said, "Deputy, that is rather an embarrassing question. If I tell you what I think, you wouldn't enjoy the speech I'd make. I'm not enjoying it a bit in here."

We talked about our various activities and I talked at some length to him about my religious convictions and finally I said, "Deputy, if we are wrong in what we teach, we are the greatest enemies of this old world that exist and every one of us ought to be in the penitentiary; but if we are telling the truth about God's Word and his purposes, and I believe we are, then God help the Government and the people who persecute us."

He folded his arms and his head dropped down. He never said a word and I got up and went out. He had not dismissed me but I thought, "If he's going to pray, I'm going to get out of here."

On the way out I met one of the officers going into the Deputy's office. The next morning I saw the same officer in the field and he said, "Come over here, Macmillan." I don't think he called me Macmillan, he said "8639, come over here." That was my number.

"What do you want, Officer?"

"What did you say to the Deputy as you were leaving the office?"

"What do you mean?"

"When you were leaving the office yesterday."

"Why, why do you ask?" I was stalling.

"Well, when I went in there I stood for a half minute, probably more, and he had his arms folded and his head bowed and never said a word to me. Finally he said, 'Macmillan is right. Macmillan is right.' Repeating it. What did you say?"

Then I told him.

PREACHING IN PRISON

The Deputy seemed really worried about the matter, and afterward he treated us with every consideration. That was quite a change from the treatment when we arrived. Our experience with the Sunday school is an instance of that. Going to church was mandatory; you couldn't get out of it unless you were sick and had a doctor's excuse or a certificate. The Catholics went in at eight and they got through at nine. We went in at 9:15 or 9:30 and got through at 10:30.

The Deputy told us when we first arrived there, "You men are in this prison for a long time. We are going to give you some work to do. Now, what can you do?"

"Deputy," I answered, "I've never done anything in my life but preach. Have you got anything like that here?"

"No, sir! That's what you are in here for, and I tell you now you are not doing any preaching here."

That was in July. Toward fall, in September, they grouped up different ones into Sunday school classes. I was given a class of about fifteen Jewish men. Judge Rutherford had a class, and Giovanni De Cecca had an Italian class. Finally we each had a class.

We were following the Quarterly Sunday school lessons and, strange to say, our lessons began with Abraham, the promises made to him and Isaac and Jacob—all the way down the line. Nothing could have been better for me to teach to a class of Jewish men.

One day I met the Deputy out on the field and he said, "Macmillan, those lessons you are having there are wonderful. I attend them all and I think that in time you will take all those Jews into the Promised Land. I'm hoping for that."

"Well," I said, "Deputy, when I came in here you told me I wasn't to do any preaching."

"Oh, forget that," he said.

The flu came along and our Sunday school was discontinued

for a time. But just before we left all the classes were united in honor of our leaving. We were going on Monday, and that Sunday Rutherford talked for about three-quarters of an hour to that group. We had a number of the officers in there and many of the men had tears running down their cheeks. They were deeply impressed. We left a little group in there that was organized to continue their study.

AN EVIDENCE OF JEHOVAH'S FAVOR

Several weeks before we were released something happened that left a deep impression on me. At New Year's time the Society held its annual election of officers in Pittsburgh. Of course Rutherford knew that those opposing the Society within the organization would come to the fore now and try to get him and all the rest of us out of office, and get a new set in whom they could run. Saturday afternoon, the first of January that year, was the time of the election. I was out at the tennis court playing. We had a tournament among the prisoners. That was the only relaxation we could get, so I was all for it.

Rutherford said, "Mac, I want to talk to you."

"What do you want to talk to me about?"

"I want to talk to you about what's going on at Pittsburgh."

"I'd like to play this tournament out here."

"Aren't you interested in what's going on? Don't you know it's the election of officers today? You might be ignored and dropped and we'll stay here forever."

"Brother Rutherford," I said, "let me tell you something perhaps you haven't thought of. This is the first time since the Society was incorporated that it can become clearly evident whom Jehovah God would like to have as president."

"What do you mean by that?"

"I mean that Brother Russell had a controlling vote and he

appointed the different officers. Now with us seemingly out of commission the matter's different. But, if we got out in time to go up to that assembly to that business meeting, we would come in there and would be accepted to take Brother Russell's place with the same honor he received. It might look then like man's work, not God's."

Rutherford just looked thoughtful and walked away.

Next morning he rapped on the cell walls and said, "Poke your hand out." He handed me a telegram saying that he had been elected president and C. A. Wise vice-president. He was very happy to see this display of assurance that Jehovah was running the Society.

That day we were in the field; the tennis tournament was over and I was quiet again. We got down to the corner and he said, "I want to tell you something. You made a remark yesterday that is working in my mind; about us being put in Brother Russell's place. It might have influenced the election and then the Lord would not have had a chance to demonstrate whom he wanted in. Why, brother, if I ever get out of here, by God's grace I'll crush all this business of creature worship if I have to get kicked out for doing it."

He was surely worked up. I sympathized with him a good deal but I did not believe he could do it. I was not counting on what was to take place in the near future.

8

A NEW NATION COMES TO LIFE

MARCH 25, 1919, we were released. We had been in the Atlanta penitentiary nine months.

Judge Howe, who had sentenced us to eighty years, denied us bail while our attorneys were preparing our case for hearing on appeal. Bail was also summarily denied by Judge Martin Thomas Manton.[1] However, our attorneys made application to United States Supreme Court Justice Louis D. Brandeis, and under his order another application was made to the Circuit Court of Appeals at New York.

Apparently the Department of Justice and Judge Howe, for reasons of their own, were extremely interested in causing withdrawal of the appeal. Our attorneys received from Howe a copy of a letter he had sent to the Attorney General at Washington, D.C., in response to a telegram the Attorney General had sent him. This letter was dated March 3, 1919, and in it he stated:

My principal purpose was to make an example, as a warning to others, and I believed that the President would relieve

them after the war was over. As I said in my telegram, they
did much damage, and it may well be claimed that they ought
not to be set at liberty so soon, but as they cannot do any
more now, I am in favor of being as lenient as I was severe
in imposing sentence. I believe most of them were sincere, if
not all, and I am not in favor of keeping such persons in confinement after their opportunity for making trouble is past.
Their case has not yet been heard in the Circuit Court of
Appeals.

CLEARED OF AN ILLEGAL JUDGMENT

However, this effort at commutation of our sentences failed
because March 21, 1919, the Circuit Court ordered that all of
us be admitted to bail in the sum of $10,000 each. Then, on
May 14 following, the court reversed the decision of the lower
court and the case was remanded for retrial. Judge Ward,
writing the opinion, said: [2] "The defendants in this case did
not have the temperate and impartial trial to which they were
entitled and for that reason the judgment was reversed."

The Court of Appeals in its decision held that it was for the
jury to decide whether or not the defendants were guilty. But
the Government didn't want to risk losing the case on another
jury trial. The prosecutor was afraid that it would be lost,
since the war hysteria that had helped the Government to convict us in 1918 no longer existed by the time the case had been
reversed in 1919. The war had ended, and prejudice was then
not so rampant. The Government was afraid that if an un-
biased jury heard the case again it would be lost. It was this
fear of losing the case that forced the Government to dismiss
the indictments by motion to *nolle prosequi*.

Occasionally since that time some of Judge Rutherford's
enemies have referred to him as an "ex-convict." Nothing
could be further from the truth, and, in view of all the well-
known evidence to the contrary, this is an obvious attempt to

prejudice persons who may not be in a position to know the facts.

If the conviction against him had not been reversed, Judge Rutherford would have been disbarred as a lawyer. An ex-convict can't be a lawyer. A lawyer who is an ex-convict must be disbarred. Yet Rutherford never lost his license.

After his erroneous conviction in 1918 Rutherford repeatedly appeared before the Supreme Court of the United States as counsel and remained a member of the bar of that court from his admission in May, 1909, until his death in 1942. Since the conviction was reversed and the stigma erased, it is wrong to say that Rutherford was an ex-convict. The facts are that he was wrongly imprisoned under an illegal judgment.

We were a happy bunch in Atlanta when a telegram came to Rutherford saying that bail had been granted. Our friends came down on Saturday so that we could leave Monday morning for New York, where arrangements for bail were completed. That weekend, of course, was a very exciting one to all of us. The guards in the prison were very kind, the Deputy warden in particular, and congratulated us on getting away.

We came to the Federal Court Building in Brooklyn, where bail was granted. It seemed very strange to walk out and go just where we wanted to without having guards shouting at us or asking us where we were going or requiring a pass.

A MARK OF CONFIDENCE

Our friends had a real "welcome home" celebration for us in New York, but now that we were out of prison we had no place to go to carry on our work. The Tabernacle was sold and the Bethel was dismantled. That of course was a blow. Practically everything was gone. We needed an office and a place where we could do a little printing.

Rutherford went to California while R. J. Martin and I

went to Pittsburgh to look at the offices where our equipment had been moved, to see if there was anything we could do. C. A. Wise was there too. He had been elected vice-president while we were in prison. We were buried on the top floor of a new building on Federal Street in Pittsburgh, and few people knew where we were. We were trying to get things going and increase the work if possible, but we were completely handicapped owing to the fact that all of our printing facilities were gone and our plates and other equipment that we needed to expand the work were destroyed. It seemed there was not a thing we could do. We would have to begin from scratch.

One morning a man walked into our office. There was no special entrance there and nobody at the door as receptionist. You could walk right into the office. I looked up from my desk and there he was—a man who had been associated with the work for many years and whom I knew well. He was a man of considerable means from one of the Southern states. He motioned for me to come out to see him and we went into a room we had fixed up as a living room or parlor.

"Who's in charge of the work here, Brother Mac," he asked.

I told him.

"Is Brother Rutherford here?"

"No, he's in California. But Brother Van is here and Brother Wise and the rest of us."

He said, "Have you got a private room here?"

"Well, we'll lock this door, this is private. What do you want to do, George?"

He began to take his shirt off as I talked to him. I thought he had gone crazy. He looked a little dirty and travel-worn, whereas ordinarily he was a tidy and well-kept man. When he got down to his undershirt he wanted a knife. Then he cut out a little patch he had on there and took out a bundle of money. It was about $10,000 in bills.

He put it down and said, "That'll help you to get this work started. I wouldn't send a check because I didn't know who

was here. I didn't travel in a sleeper because I didn't want anybody to come and take this away from me if they suspected
I had it, so I sat up all night. I didn't know who was in charge
of the work, but now that I see you brothers here whom I
know and I trust, I am glad that I came!"

"Well, George, you sure look like you had a hard time but
we're certainly glad that you came too." It was a pleasant surprise and certainly an encouragement. Eventually funds began
to come in when it became known that Rutherford was back
in his position as president and the rest of us were busy at
work with the same old organization getting started again. But
that really did not take place until after we got back to the
Bethel in New York.

A TEST OF STRENGTH IS MADE

In the meantime Rutherford, in California, decided to try a
test to see if the work could be revived, or if it might be indicated that our work was already done. Some of us were still
ready to go to heaven right away. We thought our characters
should be developed just about right after we had, in a way,
spent "eighty years" in the penitentiary. We thought we
would surely be ready then, if we had not been in 1914.

However, Rutherford was anxious about the work. He was
just in his prime, and he could not figure out why the Lord
would make such extensive preparation in starting a great
work of this kind and then letting it stop without accomplishing any more than had been done up to this time. If matters
had come to a climax after World War I, and Armageddon
had really been due to begin then, we would have been satisfied. We would have said, This is the end. But the war was
over. The nations had patched up an armistice and it looked
as if they were going to have peace. Now what were we going
to do about it? We were not going to sit around idle and

twiddle our thumbs waiting for the Lord to take us to heaven. We realized we would have to get busy and do something to determine what the Lord's will in the matter really was.

Rutherford announced that on Sunday, May 4, 1919, he would lecture in Clune's Auditorium on Fifth and Olive Streets in Los Angeles. The advertised subject of his talk was: "The Hope for Distressed Humanity." Newspaper advertising called attention to our illegal conviction with the promise that the reasons for it would be explained. That was the test case. If nobody came to that meeting, we were done.

It was reported to us that some of the clergy had said, "There won't be a soul there to hear it. Perhaps a few tramps will go in. The International Bible Students and the Watch Tower are done." I suppose from the looks of things they had every reason to believe that.

Rutherford was at the Trinity Hotel waiting. Within about twenty minutes after they opened the doors of the auditorium that place was so jammed you could not get another person in. About 3,500 had turned out to hear the talk.

Well, there it was. Of course Rutherford was thrilled. He hurried down to the auditorium and that day he really talked! About 600 had been turned away with a promise that an overflow meeting would be held on Monday night. Although Rutherford had been ill in bed all day Monday, he went to the auditorium that night to talk to the 1,500 assembled, but after about an hour he had to give up and an associate completed his lecture.

For several weeks he was in serious condition and we thought he might not survive. Due to his weakened condition he had contracted pneumonia. The doctors said his trouble was due to the poisons in his system from impure air and poor food while in the Atlanta penitentiary. He and Van Amburgh were in a cell that had no circulation of air. There was something wrong with the fan and, not getting enough oxygen, their systems became filled with poisons. At any rate he was seriously ill and never fully recovered.

NEW LIFE STIRS US TO ACTION

By July Rutherford was back to work and right then arrangements were made for an assembly at Cedar Point, Ohio, and scheduled for the first of September.

What a thrilling time that was! We had not known what to expect. The public season closed that year on September 1 and we had arranged with the hotels to take possession of all their facilities on noon that day. The week before this the weather had been very unsettled with much rain, but Monday dawned fair and clear. On Monday morning our people began to arrive and when the convention began there were about a thousand present.

The hotels at Cedar Point accommodated approximately three thousand and we had hoped to fill them, so we were somewhat disappointed at this small beginning. However, later in the day special trains began to come in and it seemed that everyone was arriving all at once. The managers of the local hotels were completely swamped. Long lines formed waiting for assignments but everyone was cheerful because it seemed so good to get together again in a general convention. We had not been able to hold such an assembly since 1916.

Martin and I volunteered to help out in assigning accommodations. I had had experience in hotel work and Martin's wide experience in office management made him valuable. We were behind the counter until after midnight, assigning rooms, while Rutherford and many of the others were having the time of their lives acting as bell boys, carrying the baggage and helping the friends get to their rooms. Everyone was thoroughly enjoying the experience and before we finished that night around three thousand persons were on the grounds and settled.

Still they continued to come. The hotels in Cedar Point were filled and overflowing into nearby Sandusky, where soon not only the hotels but hundreds of private homes also were filled. By Friday six thousand were in attendance, and Sunday at the public lecture delivered by J. F. Rutherford there were seven thousand persons present.

This was the evidence of an organization truly come to life! If our enemies had had their way we would still have been in the penitentiary, just beginning our twenty-year internment. Now, instead of that, here we were—free—finally realizing that there was a real work ahead of us, and eager to get at it.

"THE GOLDEN AGE" COMES INTO VIEW

Announcement was made of the release of a new magazine as a companion to *The Watch Tower*, which was to be published twice a month and which was to be called *The Golden Age*.

In his talk to the convention when he announced the release of the new magazine, J. F. Rutherford answered a question that was in many minds as to our future activity. He said: [3]

Faithful followers of the Master . . . know that soon they must finish their course and pass off the earthly stage of action; and yet they know there is something, by God's grace, that they will be privileged to do, and, if faithful to him, will do, before they pass over. Beyond the time of trouble by the eye of faith they see the Golden Age of the glorious reign of the Messiah, which will bring peace and the blessings of life, liberty and happiness to the groaning creation of earth. They count it as their chief duty and privilege to announce to the world the coming of the Golden Age. It is part of their God-given commission. . . .

St. Paul said: "Woe is me if I preach not the Gospel." We are sure that he here expressed the heart sentiment of every child of God who has the opportunity of proclaiming the message. The door of opportunity is opening before you. Enter it quickly. Remember as you go forth in this work [with the new magazine] you are not soliciting merely as the agent of a magazine, but you are an ambassador of the King of kings and Lord of lords, announcing to the people in this dignified manner the incoming of the Golden Age, the glorious kingdom of our Lord and Master, for which true Christians have hoped and prayed for many centuries. You are an angel of peace, bearing to a war-torn, sin-sick, sorrowing and broken-hearted world the glad message of salvation. How wonderful is our privilege!

We had truly come to life and were looking forward to years of work if necessary in order to fulfill our commission. Many of the discourses at this assembly were on service themes. The talk which I gave on Thursday highlighted the words of Jesus when he was on trial before Pilate: [4]

"To this end was I born, and for this purpose came I into the world, to bear witness to the truth." These words of our Lord Jesus to Pilate at the time of his trial set forth one of the main objects of Christ's life. The Master here showed with clearness that one of the main objects of his advent into the world was not to delve into Jewish politics, not to spend his time in various moralistic and humanitarian works, great and admirable though such works would be, but to bear testimony to the truth concerning God's aims and purposes for the blessing of mankind. It is true there were other objects in his leaving the heavenly glory which he had with the Father before the world was: he came to "seek and to save that which was lost"; he came to "give himself a ransom for man"; but his bearing witness to the truth was almost inseparably bound up with those exalted missions.

That kingdom, the true testimony of which the Lord bore and which true testimony he passed on to the apostles and through them to his faithful followers of this Gospel age, will prove to be the very thing which man has wanted and needed all along. It will be the "desire of all nations." For the privilege of testifying to that message our Lord and all his faithful followers have counted shame, ignominy, imprisonment, persecutions and death as nothing. If they called the Master of the house Beelzebub for his faithfulness in declaring the Messianic kingdom and for the things necessarily associated with that declaration, it need not be surprising if they apply similar epithets to his followers who are, of course imperfect and much more likely to call forth the criticism of the enemies of the truth.

WORLD-WIDE PREACHING IS THE GOAL

So the idea began to take hold, "Now we have something to do." We were not going to stand around any more and wait to go to heaven; we were going to work. The clear demonstration of growing interest that was manifested in our message at Clune's Auditorium the preceding May made us realize the people did want to hear why we were so opposed, and what kind of hope we had that could make us persist in spite of it. Then we began to realize a truly world-wide preaching campaign was ahead of us. The response at our convention also demonstrated that our people were eager to go ahead with it. With this thought of increased activity in mind we set out to move headquarters back to Brooklyn, New York. It took some work to refurnish Bethel and equip our offices there, but by the first of October, 1919, we were beginning to operate. *The Watch Tower* was beginning to look as it had before. Rutherford's articles were being printed again, and our people began to respond with voluntary contributions in a fairly liberal way. It was remarkable how the Lord was providing just what was needed and thus we were able to spread out and increase our activity.

Charles Taze Russell (1852-1916). President of the Watch
Tower Bible and Tract Society (1884-1916).

Joseph Franklin Rutherford (1869-1942). President of the
Watch Tower Bible and Tract Society (1916-1942).

Nathan Homer Knorr. President of the Watch Tower
Bible and Tract Society since 1942.

Fred William Franz, Vice-President of the Society since 1945.

Board of Directors of the Watch Tower Bible and Tract Society of Pennsylvania. (*Left to right*) Lyman Swingle, Thomas J. Sullivan, Grant Suiter (Sec'y.-Treas.), Hugo Riemer, Nathan H. Knorr (President), Fred W. Franz (Vice-President), Milton G. Henschel.

Hayden C. Covington *(left)*, general counsel for Jehovah's witnesses, reminisces with the author about the legal battles won in favor of freedom of worship.

Giovanni De Cecca, who was imprisoned in 1918 with the author, and who now is translator of Italian on the Headquarters staff, discusses a technical point with the linotype operator for the Italian editions of *The Watchtower* and *Awake!*

Grant Suiter, Secretary-Treasurer of the Society *(left)*, and the author in the lobby of Bethel, as workers return from the factory for the noon meal.

The morning Bible discussion in the dining hall of Bethel.

"Bethel," international headquarters of the Watch Tower Bible and Tract Society, Brooklyn, N.Y.

Brooklyn, N. Y., printing plant of the Society, with the thirteen-story addition completed in the fall of 1956.

The first issue of *The Watchtower* (center)—circulation 6,000—and changes in its format to the present—circulation over 3,000,000.

The *Golden Age* magazine (published from 1919 to 1937) was succeeded by *Consolation* (from 1937 to 1946) and is now published as *Awake!*, with a circulation by 1957 of over 2,000,000.

Watchtower Bible School of Gilead, located at South Lansing, N. Y.

Canadian Branch Office of Jehovah's witnesses at Toronto, completed in 1956.

Strathfield, New South Wales, Australia.

Copenhagen, Denmark.

Havana, Cuba.

Bombay, India.

Assembly in Hitler's former parade ground, Nuremberg, Germany, August 14, 1955, with 107,423 in attendance.

Assembly in Yankee Stadium, New York, July 26, 1953, with 116,802 in attendance. An overflow attendance of 49,027 listened in Dunellen, N. J., by direct line.

After our convention in 1919 *The Watch Tower* really began to emphasize the service for everybody. At first, a group of about seven thousand within the congregational organization carried on the bulk of the witness work. These had been active in distributing the seventh volume and now this small group reorganized and began to press forward again in their ministry.

Later *The Watch Tower* commented on Jesus' commandment,[5] "And this gospel of the kingdom shall be preached in all the world for a witness unto all nations; and then shall the end come." It was pointed out: [6]

After the fiery experiences coming upon the church, and after admonishing his followers to endure cheerfully to the end, he then specifically states the general work that must be done throughout Christendom. . . . It will be noted he does not say the gospel that has been preached to the meek throughout the entire Gospel age shall be preached. What gospel then could he mean? The gospel means good news. The good news here is concerning the end of the old order of things and the establishment of Messiah's kingdom. It means the dark night of sin and sorrow is passing away. It means that Satan's empire is falling, never to rise again. It means the sun of righteousness is rising rapidly, its healing beams penetrating the darkness and driving back that which obscures the truth and bringing to the people that which will bless, comfort, strengthen and uplift them. It means the coming in of the Golden Age, the glorious time of which all the prophets wrote and of which the Psalmist sang songs of gladness and hope. . . . Plainly this would seem to indicate that now the church must engage in the proclamation of this good news as a witness to the nations of earth, and then the old order will entirely pass away and the new will be here. Surely there could be no tidings so good, no news so comforting and helpful to the peoples of earth in this time of distress. Evidently this verse means that the witness must be given to the nations designated as Christendom. All of Christendom is now in distress and perplexity. They have experienced great trouble, but there is even greater trouble yet to come. Before that greater trouble comes, this message must go to the people as a testimony.

Here, clearly defined, is the first official expression of the world-wide preaching work as it is now actually being carried out. Here, in its issue of July 1, 1920, *The Watch Tower* was pointing to the commission that has served as the dynamic stimulus for all of Jehovah's witnesses from that time forward.

PUBLICITY AGENTS FOR THE KINGDOM OF HEAVEN

Unmistakable as those words were, our commission was to become even clearer, and with it, our responsibility was to be sharpened. This was at another convention in Cedar Point, Ohio, September 5 to 13, 1922. The talk was J. F. Rutherford's.[7]

After explaining that Jesus Christ would occupy the throne appointed by God he pointed out that God had arranged for others to be associated with him as kings, and these would rule with him for a thousand years. Preparation for these had begun when he was on earth and God had been selecting them from that time forward. However, when Jesus was due to return and take up his power as King, he would gather together the last of those on earth of this group and prepare them for the work they were to do. Then the Lord would suddenly appear at his temple [i.e., the organization built of human "stones"[8]] for a judgment of those in line for the Kingdom to determine which were faithful to their covenant.[9] From Isaiah's prophecy[10] he showed that even these faithful ones would be found in a spiritually unclean condition and would have to have their lips cleansed as with fire in the prophecy. This called for a great change in the work, and a witness for the kingdom began in earnest.

Then he quoted from Isaiah 43:8–12, "Ye are my witnesses, saith the Lord, and my servant whom I have chosen," and pointed out:

> Thus we see that those of the temple class are clearly designated as the Lord's witnesses at this time, to bring a message of consolation to the people, that the Kingdom of heaven is here, and that millions now living will never die. Thus it is seen that God purposes that his name shall be magnified, that the people shall know that he is Lord. Thus we see that God purposes to have a people in the earth in this time of stress, clearly marked as separate and distinct from all others, standing as his witnesses, fearlessly crying out the message: "The kingdom of heaven is at hand!" . . .
>
> For six thousand years God has been preparing for this kingdom. For nineteen hundred years he has been gathering out the kingdom class from amongst men. Since 1874 the King of glory has been present; and during that time he has conducted a harvest and has gathered unto himself the temple class. Since 1914 the King of glory has taken his power and reigns. He has cleansed the lips of the temple class and sends them forth with the message. The importance of the message of the kingdom cannot be overstated. It is the message of all messages. It is the message of the hour. It is incumbent upon those who are the Lord's to declare it. The kingdom of heaven is at hand; the King reigns; Satan's empire is falling; millions now living will never die. . . . The world must know that Jehovah is God and that Jesus Christ is King of kings and Lord of lords. This is the day of all days. Behold, the King reigns! You are his publicity agents. Therefore advertise, advertise, advertise, the King and his kingdom!

Suddenly, as these words filled the auditorium, a platform-length banner was unfurled that echoed the stirring phrase: "Advertise the King and Kingdom."

A mighty shout went up from the assembly. Here was our answer. No more could we doubt what Jehovah God would have us do. Gone was any question as to whether we would be working or "going home soon." The privilege and duty of all those dedicated to Jehovah's service was to advertise the presence of the Lord and to publicize his kingdom, now definitely known to be established since 1914. This we must declare world-wide if we would prove our love and loyalty to the Lord.

THE NEW WORLD SOCIETY IS BORN

Thus, was our work revived.[11] It was more than an old work coming to new life. In the fall of 1919 a new nation was born. It was the New World society of Jehovah's witnesses.

It did not all come at once. Conceived under trying conditions from its inception in 1872, it was almost brought to a stillbirth by the pains of travail from 1914 to 1918. Only Jehovah's healing hand was able to deliver it to vigorous life. Growth has been steady though fraught with tribulations and the rate of increase has multiplied in recent years.

With the regathering of Jehovah's people after their death-like inactivity in 1918–1919, the germ of theocratic structure was implanted. At that time the Society began appointing one person from each congregation to represent it directly in organizing the new work of witnessing with *The Golden Age*. Then, after we moved back to New York in 1919 we found the quarters at 124 Columbia Heights insufficient, so we expanded to 35 Myrtle Avenue, where we got several floors of a building to work on and where we installed a large printing press to print *The Golden Age*. Finally that building was too small. In 1922 we moved to 18 Concord Street, where we had four stories. Within four years we were spilling out the doors and windows again. We realized then that we would have to build our own factory.

In 1926 we purchased some ground at 117 Adams Street and

that winter erected an eight-story printing plant. In 1937 a four-story addition was made and in 1949 a nine-story annex was built. These were all joined as though they were one building. In 1956 a completely new thirteen-story building was constructed across the street that doubled all of these facilities up to that time.

These have been remarkable years. When I look back on our experiences since we entered Atlanta penitentiary in 1918 I am more than ever convinced that Jehovah God is with us. Sentenced to twenty years, with animosity against us so strong we could not obtain bail during appeal; expecting to end our days in prison; seeing the organization we had helped to build violently throttled to death—then, within *one year's time*, released and completely cleared of all stigma flowing to us from our conviction, with the strength of our early planting shown in the immediate restoration of vigorous activity—to me, this is a miracle of Jehovah, evidence that the planting was not man's but God's, revived by him to grow even more, with his spirit bringing the increase.

Yes. It is the spirit of Jehovah that moves his people. But remnants of creature worship and human adulation still remained after the internal rebellion in 1917. These must be completely cleared out if the Society of Jehovah's witnesses was to be wholly dedicated to God's service. Rutherford struck at the very heart of this structural weakness.

CHAPTER 9

JEHOVAH CHOOSES
AND CLEANSES HIS CHANNEL

J. F. RUTHERFORD's interest after leaving the penitentiary was to get the Society back on its feet and intensify the preaching work. But he had another purpose. Before he left Atlanta he had determined to rid the organization of creature worship. This he set about to do, and struck deep at the shackles still binding us to false forms of worship. That is why I think I should digress from my historical account for just a little to show you the change in attitude that has taken place with Jehovah's witnesses as regards the channel God is using to disseminate his truth.

C. T. Russell had grown up with the Society. In fact, during his lifetime he was the Society. However, I would not want you to think he magnified his own importance. He did not. He appreciated to the full the responsibility that he had, but took no credit to himself for his position or the results of this work. Still it is quite reasonable that those associated with him would drift into the attitude they did relative to his position. My own experience was similar to many others. On one occasion when I was quite young, as I remember, I went into Russell's study, looked around and said: "Brother Russell, those things that you explain in *The Watch Tower* and the literature are so wonderful; it seems to me no man could figure them out. Are you ever visited by angels here in your study to explain these things to you?"

He looked a little curious and rather amused, and said, "No, no, brother, everything necessary for us to know is in the Bible." He put his hand on his Bible. "I'm a student of prophecy, but not a prophet. God is blessing our efforts now and unfolding these truths as they are due to be understood. And as we continue to study and work, the light will increase and grow brighter." That settled my mind, of course; but I still had that lurking suspicion that perhaps he had dreams or visions of some kind.

RUSSELL VIEWED AS THE CHANNEL

You are well aware of how most people view the leaders in their religious organization. The religions with which all of us had been associated had so thoroughly trained us to look up to individuals, we didn't really at that time think of divorcing ourselves from such an attitude. Some would occasionally say to Russell: "Brother Russell, we wish we knew as much about God's Word as you do." He would reply: "If you do not know as much about it as I do, it is your own fault, because everything I know I put into print for you to read. I may know it a little sooner than you do, but sooner or later you'll get the same information. You must keep on studying." That was his view.

His effort to minister and be of service to those associated with him in the work was tireless. That is one of my lasting impressions of the man. When I talked to Russell at the assembly in Cleveland in 1901 and he invited me to make my home at Bethel, I readily accepted his invitation and returned to Allegheny with him that night by train.

Russell had given three talks that Sunday. He had spoken in the morning with the conventioners, in the afternoon he had delivered his public lecture, and at night a sort of parting message to the assembly. In those days public meetings would sometimes last two hours. When we got on the train the car was full of returning conventioners. It was brightly illuminated and everyone was talking and laughing and I could see Russell was quite tired. At about 12:30, getting on to one o'clock, I went up to where he was seated in a double seat and said, "Brother Russell, you must be very tired after this strenuous day's work and the number of people that have been visiting with you here since we got on the train. Now the next car ahead of us is a sleeping car and there's a lower berth there with fresh clean linen all ready for you to slip into and lie down. Why don't you go in and rest tonight?"

"No, brother, I'd rather stay with the friends here, thank you. It's very thoughtful of you, but I just want to stay with the friends. If the friends must stay up all night, so shall I."

That made a lasting impression on my mind. Here was a great man, as I viewed him—serving Almighty God in a way that nobody else on earth was serving him at that time, and yet he was so anxious to minister to those who were looking for information about God that he was willing to work hard all day and then sit up all night if necessary giving more detailed instruction to those who were feeling after God if haply they might find him. Others were impressed in the same way. So, while Russell himself would never elevate his position in relation to the rest of us, it was an easy matter for us to conclude that he was a special servant.

We found two places in the Hebrew Scriptures and two

places in the Christian Greek Scriptures that seemed to support the thought that Russell personally was the channel the Lord was using to dispense his truths. Russell did not make it so, but most of the rest of us did; and if anybody denied that he was that special servant we looked at him a little askance and thought he was not fully in accord with our work and did not understand matters properly.

One of those texts was in Ezekiel [1] where it speaks of the man with the inkhorn, clothed in linen, marking the foreheads of the people. That certainly pictured a work, but it was not, as we later saw, an individual's work.

Then we found at Zechariah the passage Jesus quoted the night before he was hanged on the tree,[2] "I will smite the shepherd, and the sheep shall be scattered." That was all Jesus quoted but we looked up the text and its context also, that said,[3] "Awake, O sword, against my shepherd, and against the man that is my fellow, saith the Lord of hosts: smite the shepherd, and the sheep shall be scattered: and I will turn mine hand upon the little ones." Well, that man who was his fellow, we argued, must be Russell. We thought he might be smitten too, and the Lord would put his power over the little ones so they would not be scattered as they were in the case of Jesus' death.

In the Christian Greek Scriptures we would turn to Matthew 24:45-47 where Jesus speaks of his "faithful and wise servant" whom he would appoint over all his goods. We felt certain this must refer to the work Russell was doing. Then we also applied Revelation 19:10 literally to Russell.

If it had not been for his own sincere, conscientious attitude toward the work he was doing, you can imagine how easily he might have been encouraged to take advantage of the reliance on him and seek to establish himself as an infallible guide to the Scriptures. His attitude to the last was just the opposite—self-effacing.

RUSSELL VIEWS THE SOCIETY AS THE CHANNEL

Russell never claimed he was the channel the Lord was using to dispense his truths. He maintained that he was only the servant who was working in the channel at the time. He did not want to think or state that he alone was the servant, or that he was a special servant above everybody else, but rather that he was the one occupying a position in the channel together with others. He often pointed out that if the one responsible for the work should prove unfaithful, he would immediately be set aside and somebody else put in his place. If a man ever thought he was the author of this truth, just that quickly he would cease to be a servant. The truth is Jehovah's, and his servants were used to give it out to others.

From the beginning of the organization of the Society this was Russell's thought. In announcing the application of the Society for a charter, he wrote in *Zion's Watch Tower*, as it was then called, in the issue of October, 1884: [4]

> It seems tolerably certain that some of the saints will be *in the flesh* during a great part at least of the "time of trouble"; and if so, there will be need of printed matter, tracts, etc., as much then, perhaps, as now, and possibly will be more heeded; for when the judgments of the Lord are "in the earth the inhabitants of the world will learn righteousness." (Isaiah 26:9) Should those at present prominently identified with the work not be the *last* to be "changed," [undoubtedly referring to himself] some interruption of the work might result; but this may be obviated by having a legal standing, granted by a State Charter.

Russell here clearly indicated that it was his thought that *the Society*, as organized in an orderly manner, would carry on the work he had begun. Often when he was asked, Who is that faithful and wise servant? Russell would reply: "Some say I am; while others say the Society is." Both statements were true; Russell was in fact the Society (in a most absolute sense), in that he directed the policy and course of the Society. He sometimes sought advice of others connected with the Society, listened to their suggestions, and then decided according to his best judgment what he believed the Lord would have him do.

Commenting on this parable of the "faithful and wise servant," he wrote in *Zion's Watch Tower* in 1904: [5]

> The implication seems to be that when the right time should come for understanding the parable, it would be clearly set forth: that at the time of the parable's fulfillment the Lord would appoint a servant in the household to bring these matters to the attention of all the servants, and that certain responsibilities would rest upon such a one respecting the dispatch of his duties. If faithfully performed, a great blessing would be his reward; and if unfaithful to his charge, severe penalties would be inflicted. The implication would be also that if faithful the servant would be continued in his service, and if unfaithful he would be dismissed and another take the position and its responsibilities.

THE "FAITHFUL AND WISE SERVANT" IDENTIFIED

The belief of some of us, that Russell was the channel, led us to think that when he died the work must be finished. But when it became evident that the work was only beginning, then someone had to carry on in his place. I have already told you about the selfish ambition for personal advancement that a few in the organization manifested and the sifting that took place then in fulfillment of Bible prophecy. The rift that developed helped us to realize that the clearness of our vision on this point must be lacking. Further careful study along these lines brought a number of truths to light and revealed to us that our attitude toward individuals was not pleasing to the Lord.

Rutherford, having seen the disastrous results of elevating

an individual, refused to have anyone look up to him as either
the pastor or channel, or the one who was to bring the truths
to the people as an individual. As early as 1923 he reminded
us that it was the Society as an organization that was responsible for carrying forward the work. He pointed out: [6]

> The word *Society* as used herein is a generic term applied
> to the body of consecrated, anointed Christians throughout
> the world engaged in the work of representing the King and
> the King's interests on earth. It is an organization for the
> purpose of doing the Lord's work in an orderly way. This
> organization has its officers, elected in an orderly manner.
> The officers are not the Society, but are servants of the Soci-
> ety. Should every individual now in the Society prove dis-
> loyal, the Lord could put others into their places, and still the
> Society would exist and continue his work. Let us be wise
> enough to make the distinction between office and individ-
> ual. All the individual members of the Society may make
> mistakes, being imperfect, but that would not mean that the
> Lord would cast off his organization and go about doing his
> work in a disorganized manner.

Later, in 1931, at London, England, Rutherford gave a talk
on the ninth chapter of Ezekiel, proving from the Scriptures
that the man with the inkhorn was not an individual.[7] He
pointed out that the other six men in that picture were
not individuals but represented Jehovah's invisible heavenly
forces that he would use to destroy Satan's organization, including false religion, at Armageddon. Now there were six
of those men with slaughter weapons and one man with the
inkhorn. If the six were symbolic of a group, then the man
with the inkhorn must likewise picture a group or an organization. So he concluded that the "faithful and wise servant"
could not be an individual, such as C. T. Russell, but was a
class of persons made up of those faithful Christians anointed
with God's holy spirit who were sharing in the commission
to preach "this good news of the kingdom."

ONE ORGANIZATION IS MADE RESPONSIBLE

All associated with the organization were enthusiastic in their reception of this understanding, and as time went on it became even more fully established. In Isaiah 43:10–12 (*American Standard Version*), it says, "Ye are my witnesses, saith Jehovah, and my servant." Although a number of witnesses are indicated, the term "servant" is in the singular. "My *servant* whom I have chosen; that ye may know and believe me, and understand that I am he." (Italics mine.) It can readily be seen that that servant is made up of many witnesses. We realized then that the chosen servant of Matthew 24:45–47 could not apply to one man, but must represent a group of faithful Christians eating the same spiritual food at the same spiritual table and all, according to Jesus' own promise, being served by him at the time of his return.[8]

It is true that in his dealings with mankind in times past Jehovah sent his truth to the people in various ways, often through individuals. Some came through Enoch and some through Noah as well as Abraham, Isaac and Jacob; but a great flood of revelations came through the channel of the nation of Israel in the days of Moses while the truth was being unfolded. Later on came the prophets and then God's own Son through whom all of his Word is now spoken.[9] Since Jesus established the early congregation there is no indication that Jehovah would especially select an individual as set apart from others. The Scriptures show clearly that he would use a visible or physical channel which Jesus called a "faithful and wise servant," whom he said he would appoint over all his "goods" or earthly interests of his Kingdom. This means there would be just one organization authorized to dispense the good news to others. So, while some headship must be exercised and Rutherford was readily accepted in that capacity, still it is the entire organization that has the responsibility, not just one man or even a small group of men at the head of the organization.

This advancing view of the channel and the proper place of individuals in the Society was a great blessing to us. It was also a source of assurance that Jehovah's purpose was to maintain his own organization and keep it clean. This was because God had put his name on his organization. That knowledge made us all the more aware of our own individual responsibilities, because we knew now more than ever that if any of us would not keep ourselves in line with Jehovah's righteous requirements, he would send his angels to gather us out of the organization.[10] And since the prophecies had so clearly foretold that only one united group would be used as a composite "servant," it meant that all other organizations would be called up for an accounting.

SINCERITY ALONE IS NOT ENOUGH

This may be difficult for you to understand. Perhaps you've always been taught that sincerity is enough. But just being sincere doesn't teach us what God's will is, does it? So no matter how "sincere" we may be or think we are, if we are associated with an organization that is not actually doing God's will, then how can we expect God to approve us? Paul said at 1 Corinthians 4:4 (*Revised Standard Version*), "I am not aware of anything against myself, but I am not thereby acquitted. It is the Lord who judges me."

Some time ago in my house-to-house preaching I met a man who raised these very objections. He said: "One thing that I can't understand or agree on with you people is your coming to the doors of regular church members like me. I have no objection to your practicing your own religion, but I have been a member of my church as long as I can remember. My parents belonged to the same church and I expect to die in this faith. So why should I be interested in changing?"

"My calling at your door is not an evidence of doubt as to your sincerity," I replied. "If I thought there were no sincere people other than Jehovah's witnesses why would I even bother to go from door to door? But belonging to an organization is not enough to gain salvation."

"I know that," he answered; "that's what my church teaches. If I don't practice my religion, I can't expect to be saved."

"But the matter goes deeper than that. I've been a minister for over fifty years and at one time or another I have talked to people from just about every religion there is, I suppose. And I've learned something first-hand that you will no doubt be willing to admit. It is that in all religions there are some, perhaps even many, who do not practice their religion sincerely. Most of them don't even know too clearly what their church teaches. Isn't that true?"

"Yes, but it's their own fault and they're the ones that will suffer for it. You don't think that God is going to condemn a religion just because some who are associated with it are insincere, do you?"

"It really isn't what you or I think about it that counts, is it? But what God himself thinks or has said he will do. Religious organizations are like nations, they are made up of people. No nation can be morally stronger or healthier than its nationals. If the ones making up that society are not individually righteous, the entire nation will be rotten to the core."

"I'm not sure I altogether agree with that conclusion," the church member stoutly contradicted. "God does not condemn the righteous with the wicked. I believe the sincere few will save the organization."

"Perhaps for a time," I agreed, "but sooner or later a time of accounting for the entire organization will come. There is an excellent example of this in the Bible you know."

"What is it?"

"It is that of the ancient commonwealth of Israel; the historical account of its birth as a nation, its entry and occupation of God-assigned territory and its rise to prominence in the ancient world."

"But how do we know that it is an example to us today?"

"Because the apostle Paul said that it was. In fact, he was speaking about the division that had already begun in the early Christian congregation and then he mentioned the various causes for deflection in the formative years of Israel and said: 'Now these things went on befalling them as examples and they were written for a warning to us upon whom the accomplished ends of the systems of things have arrived.' [11] Are you familiar with that account of Moses and the Israelites in the wilderness?"

"I remember reading about it in Sunday school. That was some time ago," he admitted.

"Then suppose we refresh our memories along the line of this point of national salvation?"

INDIVIDUAL RESPONSIBILITY DEMONSTRATED

"When the Israelites were slaves in Egypt and Jehovah God sent Moses as his servant to deliver them, they left Egypt en masse. They went out by entire families, taking with them even people of the land who manifested interest in their God. It was not difficult for them to go, viewing the matter in one way, because there was some strength in their great multitude. Since it is believed there were at least two million people in that exodus, it can be seen that it would be much easier for a member of a family to go along than to remain behind."

"It's always easier to go along with the crowd."

"That's the point. But they all didn't go out with full faith in the delivering arm of Jehovah. That was soon clearly demonstrated. Before they had reached the Red Sea some began to complain and show fear. After they were again miraculously delivered and had witnessed the destruction of Pharaoh's pursuing army in the sea, they still failed to maintain unbroken solidarity in worship. They flagrantly flouted the simple requirements of Jehovah and brought on themselves a speedy purge that God commanded Moses and a few faithful followers to execute.

"Again, in spite of these experiences, the nation balked when the way of entry into the land of promise lay open to them. Again they demonstrated lack of faith and displayed fear instead. For this evidence of spiritual rottenness Jehovah required them to wander in the wilderness for forty years. All of those, with a few exceptions, who had been over twenty on leaving Egypt soon died by the way and were left literally to rot in the desert. Now that the spiritual strength of the nation was thus renewed it was permitted to enter and occupy the land. Aside from the second generation of those leaving Egypt, only a carefully selected faithful few were permitted to attain what all had sought through the Exodus."

SPARED FOR GOD'S NAME'S SAKE

"But the nation was delivered in spite of the fact that most of them died."

"Yes, the nation was delivered, but not because of the few who remained faithful. Moses warned the small remnant of survivors and the new generation of this in a discourse he made to them just before they entered the land. He said, 'It was not because of your being the most populous of all the peoples that Jehovah showed affection for you so that he chose you, for you were the least of all the peoples. But it was because of Jehovah's loving you and because of his keeping the sworn statement that he had sworn to your forefathers that Jehovah brought you out with a strong hand, that he might redeem you from the house of slaves, from the hand of Pharaoh the king of Egypt. And you well know that Jehovah your God . . . will not hesitate toward the one who hates him. He will repay him to his face.' [12] In the Psalms it shows further why God preserved the Israelites. It says, 'Nevertheless he saved them for his name's sake, that he might make his mighty power to be known.' " [13]

"What you are saying is that God saved them only because of his promise to their forefathers and because he had put his name on them."

"That's right; the Bible says that."

"Then you believe that if the organization does not have God's name it will not be spared for the sake of those in it who may be faithful or sincere?"

"Yes, that's my point. You see, true worship is an individual matter. 'Following the crowd' or the 'family religion' did not bring salvation to those of Israel. And even the few faithful ones did not save the nation, even though God had put his name on it. Eventually, because of the extent of their apostasy in the days of Jesus, the nation was completely rejected and God withdrew his name from it. Then A.D. 70 the nation was destroyed by the Romans, and only a small remnant of those who clung to Judaism escaped. But even these were not shown favor. Until just a few years ago the nation has not been in existence, but even now modern Israel admittedly has not returned to the government of the Mosaic Law Covenant. Only those, in Jesus' day, who completely separated themselves from the traditions of the Jewish apostasy were preserved by God. It was to these that he demonstrated a new way of life and later they were joined by faithful persons from many other nations on an equal footing in the Christian congregation."

APOSTASY BEGAN IN THE EARLY CONGREGATION

"Well I think I can agree with what you've said; but, of course, I believe that God has put his name on my church. It has survived all these centuries, and yours has only come up in the last generation. Why should I believe that you are right? Doesn't the Bible say that false prophets will arise?"

"Yes it does. But the fact that a religion has survived for centuries does not of itself make that religion true. Already in the days of the early congregation the apostasy had begun. The apostle Paul called this to the attention of the Corinthians in his first letter and warned them against the divisions that had begun to arise in the congregation over doctrine.[14] Even before that he had cautioned the Galatians about being drawn away by another good news that was being preached and reminded them that 'a little yeast ferments the whole lump.' It seems that even after the governing body had settled the question of circumcision, some were still resisting and trying to establish a teaching of their own.[15] Still later Paul wrote Timothy a warning against two men who were teaching a false doctrine about the resurrection and he pointed out their false teaching 'will spread like gangrene.' [16]

"Then Paul wrote a letter about this to the Thessalonians. This was the second letter he had written, because in the first he had been discussing the second coming of Christ and some had read into his words that Jesus' presence was imminent. So he wrote to them to correct that false impression and said: 'Let no one seduce you in any manner, because it will not come unless the falling away comes first and the man of lawlessness gets revealed.' Then he added these words: 'True, the mystery of this lawlessness is already at work.' [17]

"So Paul pointed out clearly that false doctrine was already beginning to work corruption within the organization and as a sort of farewell warning to the overseers of the congregation at Ephesus he said: 'I know that after my going away oppressive wolves will enter in among you and will not treat the flock with tenderness, and from among yourselves men will rise and speak twisted things to draw away the disciples after themselves. Therefore keep awake.' [18]

"You see, Paul did not believe the falling away or the arising of false prophets would wait until the last days. He showed it had already begun. Apparently by the end of the first century some had already begun to teach that Jesus was part God while on earth because John, just before he died, wrote: 'Many deceivers have gone forth into the world, persons not confessing Jesus Christ as coming in the flesh. This is the deceiver and the antichrist.' [19]

"Now the conclusion of the matter is this. Jehovah God does not change in principle. He has no more reason now to approve a religion indiscriminately of its adherents than he did centuries ago in the wilderness of Sinai. Jehovah's witnesses do not believe that he will do so."

BEING SURE OF THE RIGHT RELIGION

"Then what do you think is the answer?"

"Jehovah's witnesses believe that the truths that have been lost through the centuries are now being restored to all kinds of people. They believe these people are being 'called . . . out of darkness into his wonderful light,' and are being associated together in an organization dedicated to God's service.[20] The only way we can be sure of our doctrine is to test it thoroughly by going to the Bible itself. Those of the early congregation did. They did not leave it to someone else to do for them. They made sure of all the things they believed, and they were approved by God.[21] That is what Jehovah's witnesses have done, too. That is why we believe we have the truth and why we call at the homes of people of all faiths," I concluded.

Have you been told that Jehovah's witnesses are narrow and bigoted for having these views? Before you make up your own mind on the matter, remember this: Jesus and all of his disciples of the first century were sure they had the right religion. They were so sure of it they were willing to oppose all the popular and so-called orthodox views of the day.[22] They were willing to persist in this course even to the point where they sacrificed their lives for it.[23]

We all live in the same world community. Therefore we should examine one another's religions even if only for the purpose of understanding our neighbors better. Besides, we should examine our own religion from time to time. The apostle Paul said: [24] "Examine yourselves, whether ye be in the faith."

To condemn a religion only because it claims to be the right one is to deny God's promise to have only "one way" and is to condemn Jesus himself who said,[25] "I am the way." True, many religions claim to be "Christian" and therefore following that "one way," but remember, Jesus said also: [26] "Not every one that saith unto me, Lord, Lord, shall enter into the kingdom of heaven; but he that doeth the *will* of my Father which is in heaven." (Italics mine.)

Jehovah God does not have many contradictory "wills." He communicates with us through one Word, the Bible. But he does not reveal his purposes separately to each individual. His one will is expressed through one channel that he himself has built up. No man can claim any credit for it. No man or group of men could accomplish its work without God's spirit. That makes it God's work.

But how does God express himself through his channel? Isn't it just a matter of interpretation of the Bible? Perhaps we'd better settle those questions, too, before I describe to you the growing pains of the new-born New World society.

CHAPTER 10

INTERPRETATION BELONGS TO GOD

You MAY HAVE heard someone say that Jehovah's witnesses interpret the Bible to suit themselves. Now most people who try to please themselves look out for their own interests and make things easy. Yet the interpretation of the Bible Jehovah's witnesses adhere to has not been an easy one to follow. Actually we do not interpret the Bible, either privately or as an organization. Remember, Jesus said concerning those who would be watching,[1] "The master . . . will gird himself and have them sit at table, and *he* will come and serve them." (Italics mine.)

That means the entire Society or family are seated at the Lord's spiritual table and all are fed together from God's Word at the hand of their Master, Jesus Christ. Although they study individually also, it is not a private matter with each one, because of their group study. In this way, since all receive individual instruction, they all become individually qualified for their ministry. Yet since they spiritually eat together at the one source, their understanding is uniform. They are not divided by conflicting private interpretations. Then how does the interpretation come?

FINDING THE HARMONY OF THE BIBLE

Not too long ago I got into a discussion with a man who had been a sincere Catholic all of his life. Our conversation on the Bible led us to a consideration of the doctrine of the trinity, and this point of interpretation came up.

"Now I'll admit," my friend said, "that the word 'trinity' does not appear in the Bible, and the Bible does not say specifically that there are three distinct personalities in the Godhead. But we Catholics believe that the Church has the authority to pronounce dogma in order to express clearly those doctrines that are not distinctly taught in the Bible."

"But how can the Catholic Church have authority to teach something that is not taught by the Bible, or that is contrary to what the Bible states?" I asked.

"Well, I don't think she teaches anything contrary to the Bible," he replied. "But if the doctrine of the trinity for example is not clearly expressed in the Scriptures, then why shouldn't the Church add her voice for the benefit of her children?"

"But that is rather dangerous, don't you think?"

"Why is it?"

"Well, assume for a moment that the Church does have that right. That doesn't leave much need for the Bible itself does it? Take this doctrine of a trinity. Of what value are all of the texts that might give light on the subject if, in the final analysis, we rely on an authority aside from the Bible for the understanding?"

"Well, I believe the Church can interpret correctly."

"Yes, because you are a Catholic. But do you think the

average Protestant would accept an interpretation just on that basis?"

"All churches claim the right to interpret the Bible. Why shouldn't the Catholic Church?"

"I don't think any organization has that right. If a group cannot demonstrate solely from the Bible that its teachings should be accepted, what basis do they have for convincing anyone outside of their own organization? It would be just one man's opinion against another's. *The Watchtower* doesn't claim to interpret the Bible. We believe that God had the Bible recorded so that in his due time a proper harmony of the Scriptures on a certain point will reveal God's own mind on the matter. That is the only correct interpretation."

"What do you mean?"

"Well, let me demonstrate it. We have just admitted that the Bible does not discuss the trinity as a doctrine. Now what is the truth in regard to the relationship of the Father and the Son? Certainly, God knows. And we have every reason to believe that the writers of the Bible must have known, too. They were inspired. Therefore their conception of the true relationship of the Father and the Son would certainly appear in their expressions when they are discussing that relationship. So we should make an effort to determine the view they had by the things they actually said, not by some interpretation that we would like to put on their words."

"Do you think that can be relied on for something as important as one of the central doctrines of the Christian church?"

"How else can we determine if it really is one of the central doctrines? You see, I still believe the Bible is sufficient. Paul wrote to Timothy,[2] 'All scripture, inspired of God, is profitable to teach, to reprove, to correct, to instruct in justice, That the man of God may be perfect, furnished to every good work.' That text says the Bible will completely equip

us with doctrine and instruction and makes no suggestion that
we need tradition outside of the Bible to complete it."

"How can you determine what any writer meant on a subject if he is not directly discussing that subject? That's where
the interpretation comes in."

"Not at all. That is where most Bible students make their
mistake, and why we have so many differing interpretations."

"How would you do it?"

"By comparing his words with another's, or with his own
when expressed in different words or from a different viewpoint."

JESUS QUOTED SCRIPTURE AS AUTHORITY

"But that is one objection that I have always had to Jehovah's
witnesses. You take Scriptures from all over the Bible and put
them together like a jigsaw puzzle. You can prove anything
that way."

"Not unless you take the Scriptures out of their proper
context. Jesus constantly quoted the words of writers of the
'Old Testament,' or Hebrew Scriptures, to establish a thought.
So did Paul and Peter. They did not rely on their own interpretation. That is the proper way to determine what a writer
meant. Why, in the Sermon on the Mount Jesus actually made
twenty-one different quotations from eight different books of
the Hebrew Scriptures [3] to establish the authority for his
doctrine. Surely you don't think he was misusing the Scriptures do you?"

"He was God. That makes a difference."

"Well, he certainly had the mind of God. And that is what
we should try to get. But we can't if we insist on attaching
meanings to his words that he never intended. Let me illustrate it by a few texts that discuss the relationship of the
Father and the Son. Take the text at John 10:30 (*Douay*).

It says, 'I and the Father are one.' Now, what does that mean to you?"

"Just what it says. The Father and the Son are one. That means they are one God."

"Well, taking the Scripture by itself it might seem that way, although it doesn't actually say they are one God, does it? In the first place, he isn't talking about the *identity* of the Father or his own *identity*. He says in verse 25: 'The *works* that I do in the name of my Father, they give testimony of me.' So he's talking about their relationship in their work, not in a 'Godhead.' But before we jump to any final conclusions and read into the text something Jesus may never have meant, suppose we turn to another place where he is also discussing his relationship to his Father. Notice here he is comparing their own relationship with that of those who would become members of his 'body.' It is at John 17:20–22, *Douay* translation. 'And not for them only do I pray, but for them also who through their word shall believe in me; That they all may be one, as thou, Father, in me, and I in thee; that they also may be one in us; that the world may believe that thou hast sent me. And the glory which thou hast given me, I have given to them; that they may be one, as we also are one.' Now, you couldn't very well say he was discussing their relationship as part of the Godhead, could you? Because then there would be more than just three in one."

"That's obvious, I believe."

"Then why do we say in the other text we just read that he was viewing his relation to his Father in that mystical way? He was talking about his works there, too, wasn't he?"

ONENESS OF JESUS WITH GOD IN THEIR WORKS

"What about the text that says, 'If you have seen me you have seen the Father.' That's plain enough, isn't it?"

"What is he talking about when he makes the statement? Notice the entire reference at John 14:8–10 (*Douay*). Here again, as in both of the other instances, Jesus is talking about the works he has done and the words he has spoken, as he says: 'The words that I speak to you, I speak not of myself. But the Father who abideth in me, he doth the works.' "

"But don't you see? He says right there that the Father abides in him."

"Let me caution you again, now. What right do we have to say he meant anything different than when he very clearly prayed to his Father and said about his disciples: 'that they all may be one, as thou, Father, *in me*, and I *in thee*; that they also may be one *in us*.' If we attach a certain meaning to his words without just cause, then we are truly wresting the Scriptures and making them subject to private interpretation."

"What do you think he meant?"

"Jesus said he did nothing without authority from the Father. This shows oneness of purpose. Besides, the one delegating authority is superior to the one receiving it, so Jesus is not equal with the Father as the doctrine of the trinity teaches.[4] In fact Jesus said,[5] 'The Father is greater than I.'

"In this point of oneness," I concluded, "I can think of no statement in the Bible which would more clearly infer that two persons could still be only *one*, than the description of a man and woman who marry. Jesus said: [6] 'For this cause shall a man leave father and mother, and shall cleave to his wife, and they two shall be in one flesh.' Now Jesus actually *says* these two become just one, yet no one would interpret his words to mean they enter into a mystical oneness similar to the 'three persons, yet one God' of the trinity. Why not? Because it is obvious he really didn't mean that. Why, then, in the face of so many statements to the contrary should we attribute such an obscure meaning to references to the oneness of the Father and the Son? Besides, none of these statements even mention a third 'person' like the 'holy ghost,' so at best it could only establish a 'duality,' and not a 'trinity.' That is why Jehovah's witnesses refuse to interpret the Bible themselves. The true meaning of any text can be determined only when it is harmonized with the rest of the Bible and in keeping with their contexts. That way, the interpretation is God's, not man's."

PROPHECY UNFOLDS WITH ITS FULFILLMENT

Now I have tried, by relating this incident to you, to demonstrate an extremely important point in this matter of interpretation. Isaiah encourages us,[7] "Come now, and let us reason together, saith Jehovah: though your sins be as scarlet, they shall be as white as snow." This makes it quite clear that we can and should reason upon such doctrines of the Bible as salvation, the trinity and other basic fundamental teachings. These foundations of Christian faith were argued by Paul and others of the early congregation, and most of these cardinal doctrines were restored early in C. T. Russell's study. Restoration was necessary because, as both Peter and Paul foretold, they would be lost.[8] Such reasoning was not done by man's wisdom, but by a comparison of scriptures under the Lord's direction until complete harmony was found for all of them without successful contradiction.

Prophecy, however, is different. The apostle Peter said: "No prophecy of Scripture springs from any private release." [9] That is, no one can "reason out" the fulfillment. We have to wait until it happens. As events occur we need only to be aware of them and be fully acquainted with the prophecies recorded. The fulfillment becomes quite clear, unless, of course, we are still not clear on the fundamentals of the Bible. As an illustration Paul wrote to the Hebrews [10] that he had some deep things to say about Jesus, how certain promises made long beforehand were fulfilled in Christ. 'But,'

Paul said, 'you still have to learn the basic teachings of Christianity again. How can you understand these deeper aspects of the prophecies about Christ,' he argued, 'if you still have to feed on the milk of God's Word?'

It was in this way that the fundamental purposes of God were revealed to that little group headed by Russell who were watching for Jesus' return. This channel the Lord has kept on using and it has grown in understanding. Points of prophecy have been obscure at times because events had not yet progressed sufficiently, but the light is getting brighter as those foretold events occur.[11] As the prophecies are fulfilled, they are studied along with the physical facts and thus they become "meat in due season" to all of those feeding at the table Jehovah, through Jesus Christ, has set for his channel, his "faithful and discreet slave." [12]

OUR VIEW OF THE NEW WORLD SOCIETY CLEARS UP

Development of our understanding of prophecies in relation to the New World society is an example of how the knowledge of God's purposes has unfolded. It was not until some years after 1919 that it was understood that there was a New World society being gathered and brought to maturity. This, we then realized, was to be carried through the battle of Armageddon as a nucleus of the new world arrangement to be set up during the thousand-year reign of Christ. We made an effort to understand it, and were able to get some important information that was helpful at the time; but the details could not be understood until God's time to fulfill the prophecy or until events were far enough advanced to see clearly the prophecies were being fulfilled.

Birth of the New World society brought changes in our thinking as well as in our activity. True, we knew that only a "little flock" [13] had been promised the kingdom of heaven.

But Revelation 7 spoke of a "great multitude" in addition to this limited number of 144,000 who compose the "little flock." [14]

Furthermore, in the seventh chapter of Revelation we have the picture of four angels holding back the four winds of the earth. This is the same condition Jesus described at Matthew 24:22 when he said: "For the elect's sake those days [of tribulation against Satan's wicked system] shall be shortened." Following the war in heaven that began in 1914, the angels of the Lord are not permitted to blow and wreck or destroy the things of this world's organizations until a certain work is done. Now what was that work? First it was the sealing of the 144,000 or completing the number of those who would make up the "little flock." Then, after that was done, John saw a great crowd or great multitude, standing before the throne, singing the praises of Jehovah and thanking him that they were delivered from the persecutions that were coming upon them. Now the question we had asked ourselves was, Who are these? And what are we to do for them? These and similar questions had puzzled Bible scholars for years.

John was told they were a group to come out of great tribulation. This and other features of the prophecy show a definite time element is involved. Therefore, an understanding of this text in Revelation 7 was not due until the time of this tribulation had begun and the time to deal with this "great multitude" had arrived. After the beginning of the period of tribulation on Satan's world which began in 1914 with the war in heaven, and after the birth of the New World society in 1919, this time had come. When these and other features of Bible prophecy began to clear up, an exhaustive study was made of all the texts and subject-matter relating to this prophecy in Revelation, and in view of conditions that had by this time developed in the organization we realized that the great crowd was composed of those who would be called by Jehovah and prepared for an everlasting home on earth in the new world. These must be gathered before Armageddon and be carried through that great battle. This understanding did not come until 1935.

Now it is clear to all in the New World society; and their hope is to be carried through the battle of Armageddon into the new world. If faithful to the principles of that new world, they will live on to everlasting life and be the "millions now living [that] will never die."

During the last ten or fifteen years, we have looked not so much for any new unfolding of doctrine, but a clearer appreciation of those prophecies already revealed. Now the light of truth is guiding us to know what to expect before Armageddon. That is something we never understood in the past. Events had not developed sufficiently. Now we know the New World society must be fully developed, and that is a world-wide work. Although some who oppose Jehovah's witnesses would like to make it appear otherwise, we do not claim, "Chronology shows the final end will come on such and such a date." The work will not end until it is completed. Matthew 24:14 says this good news of the kingdom will be preached in all the world as a witness to the nations, and *then* the end will come.

This principle of interpretation was stated many centuries ago in Egypt. Joseph, a faithful worshiper of Jehovah, answered two officers of the Pharaoh when they were puzzled because no one could reveal to them the meaning of their dreams. He said,[15] "Do not interpretations belong to God?" Then, under inspiration, he explained to them what the future held in store.

Even Daniel, the prophet, was made to realize that prophecy can be understood only in God's due time. He reports: [16] "And I heard, but I understood not: then said I, O my lord, what shall be the issue of these things? And he said, Go thy way, Daniel; for the words are shut up and sealed till the time of the end. Many shall purify themselves, and make themselves white, and be refined; but the wicked shall do wickedly; and none of the wicked shall understand; but they that are wise shall understand."

RESISTING GOD'S INTERPRETATION LEADS TO DISASTER

Development of understanding of God's purposes has been progressing since the days of the early congregation. Even the disciples of Jesus did not receive all their understanding during his presence with them. In fact, when the holy spirit was poured out on them at Pentecost they did not have it all. They had only one clear point at Pentecost, and that is that God would select a people for his name from among the nations—first the Jews. And how difficult it was for them later to see that any Gentiles would be taken in. Why, some rebelled against it. "No Gentile can come in," they argued; "if he's going to be one of us he'll have to be circumcised and keep the law." The apostle Paul had quite a time straightening them out. It was such an important matter that they went to Jerusalem to the governing body of the entire church and thrashed it out for several days before they had it cleared up.[17]

It was even after this that Paul had to clear up a point for Peter while he was visiting in Antioch. Peter had been conducting himself as a Gentile in regard to the Law until certain Jewish Christians arrived. Then he began to keep certain features of the Law by separating himself from the Gentile Christians. Paul asked him: [18] "If you, though you are a Jew, live as the nations do, and not as Jews do, how is it that you are compelling people of the nations to live according to Jewish practice?" Obviously Peter was not "infallible," even in this matter of faith and morals.

As the truth unfolded gradually to the early congregation, so the truth is gradually unfolding itself today. As some became offended and dropped out then,[19] so do some today.

They got themselves into a rut by saying, "Now this is as far as we'll go. Accepting these advanced ideas involves too much change." The "popular" religions of Christendom have done just that. They drew up a creed and said, "That creed will show that we have not slipped away and gotten into error."

Instead the creed has kept them from going along in the increasing light of truth. The rut has become a chasm with its dead end at Armageddon.

CHAPTER 11

BUILT ON A PRIMITIVE FOUNDATION

Birth of the New World society in 1919 brought changes in our thinking and in our activity. The period that followed was a time of constant change and development. Strengthened by our trying experiences during World War I, we were beginning to take firm root among people of all nations. But we were not a part of this present system of things. Therefore, this world could not understand our position or our aims.

Even though we had been cleared of an illegal judgment of seditious conspiracy, we were viewed with suspicion and distrust from all sides. The systems of this world were well established and set in their own pattern of activity. They viewed us as "new," as an "upstart" society, and our doctrine as "radical" and "impractical." The chasm which separated us was of their making. They wanted it that way and resented any interference.

J. F. Rutherford, however, was not a man to "pull his punches." He spoke as simply and directly to the people as he knew how, and he was an extremely forthright man. He was thoroughly convinced that what he had to say was the truth and that it was a matter of life and death.

As was the case with Russell, it had not taken Rutherford long to realize that the religions of Christendom were drifting further away from the principles and truth of the Bible. Many of the Protestant religions were turning to higher criticism of the Bible, and in a quiet, underhanded way were destroying the confidence of the people in the inspiration of the Bible as the guide for daily living. To many it had become a book of philosophy. Catholicism had always taken the view that the Bible was not sufficient to guide people in worship or in the affairs of life, and had to add tradition to it. Expensive church buildings, the collection plate, high-salaried clergy, church bazaars, raffles and bingo parties—none of which were employed in early Christian worship—all smacked of materialism and strengthened Rutherford's resolve to emphasize a simple form of worship that involved individual dedication to God and to his service.

Rutherford repeatedly charged the leaders of Christendom: "You are commercializing religion and making salvation just a business proposition, a matter of money, rather than a matter of devotion to Jehovah in covenant relationship with him." It was not just condemning someone else's religion. God's name was involved and so was the individual destiny of everyone on earth. So he was justified in his position and he was fired with enthusiasm in proclaiming it.

Of course, his plain unvarnished speech made him many enemies, and when his slogan, "Religion is a snare and a racket," began to appear their teeth were bared in earnest. What our enemies had failed to accomplish in 1918 some of them now determined must be done. A well-organized campaign was set in motion to discredit, undermine and completely destroy our work of preaching the good news of the Kingdom.

RUTHERFORD BEGINS TO UNIFY OUR WORK

Meanwhile, Rutherford realized we were too loosely organized for any concerted effort of our own. With the birth of the New World society in 1919 a new spirit had come into us and we were eager to carry our message of Jehovah's established kingdom to the ends of the earth. This meant we must close up our ranks and unify our efforts.

Russell had left it much to the individual as to how we were to fulfill our responsibilities. When we were sent out as speakers to visit the congregations we had our own way about it. We selected our own subjects for our talks and, as a result, there was considerable confusion as to what was said. Rutherford wanted to unify the preaching work and, instead of having each individual give his own opinion and tell what he thought was right and do what was in his own mind, gradually Rutherford himself began to be the main spokesman for the organization. That was the way he thought the message could best be given without contradiction. At the same time we began to realize that each one of us had a responsibility to go from house to house and preach.

We were shown that it was a covenant-keeping arrangement. We had a duty to God, as well as a privilege and a duty to our fellow-men to see that they were informed of God's purposes. God's favor and approval was not to be won by developing "character." In 1927 we were shown that the way each individual was to serve was to go from door to door. Sunday especially was stressed as the most opportune day to find the people at home.

What a furor that started! Even within the organization a few objected. "I couldn't go to the door on Sunday morning and offer someone literature," they said. "People would think I was breaking the Sabbath. I'll stay home and I'll prepare a nice sermon in the morning and in the afternoon or evening

I'll dress up in my frock coat and wing collar and I'll come up and give them a good talk and that will be serving the Lord." That was the position a few of the elders took. The majority, though, recognized it was the way Jesus and the apostles did the work and took it up gladly.

PREACHING THE LORD'S WORD ON THE LORD'S DAY

The reaction of some of the householders whom we approached was interesting, to say the least. One of Jehovah's witnesses I had known for some time was a prominent businessman and well known in the community where he lived. On Sunday morning he appeared at a lady's home with some Bible study aids, offering them for a small contribution, and the lady of the house took him to task.

"Mr. Cuppett," she said, "I'm astonished to see a man of your standing coming to people's homes on Sundays trying to sell something. There are six days in the week that you could do this selling and not today."

"Well," he said, "Mrs. Knox, if you can show me from the Lord's Word that it's wrong to do the Lord's work on the Lord's day, I'll quit and go home."

That took her by surprise and she stopped and reasoned with him on the matter. He reminded her of the fact that Jesus performed works of healing on the sabbath day and it seemed to the Pharisees looking on that he was desecrating the sabbath. Cuppett opened his Bible and read to her: [1] "There was a certain man before him which had the dropsy. And Jesus answering spake unto the lawyers and Pharisees, saying, Is it lawful to heal on the sabbath day? And they held their peace. And he took him, and healed him, and let him go; And answered them, saying, Which of you shall have an ass or an ox fallen into a pit, and will not straightway pull him out on the sabbath day? And they could not answer him again to these things."

Then Cuppett said: "I'm calling on you for a good purpose. Like that poor son of Abraham that Jesus cured, most of the people in the world today are in a worse condition than the ox or ass that falls into a pit. We're not performing physical cures today, but the spiritual healing that is available through these Bible study aids I am offering you is far more important. This information will show you and your family how to find lasting security for the future."

Mrs. Knox was like a number of people we used to meet, more so in the past than in recent years. She had become so used to thinking of religion only in connection with a certain type of building and service that she could not understand how someone could call at her home with anything truly religious. If it wasn't done the way it was done in her church, then there must be something wrong with it, she argued. She thought nothing of her minister passing the collection plate on Sunday to pay his salary and otherwise finance her religion, but when Cuppett offered her a printed sermon at her door for a contribution just to cover the printing cost, it became something commercial to her mind. She didn't realize that Cuppett wasn't even being paid for his work. In fact, it was actually costing him money to visit her home. But when he explained how Jesus carried on his work, then she was willing to take some of his books and look into the matter.

While this extensive house-to-house ministry met with an immediate response, a small minority seriously objected. Most of these were influenced by their clergymen and determined to put a stop to our work. They stirred up the police and within a few months after our special Sunday activity began, the first arrest occurred at South Amboy, New Jersey. That was in 1928.

DANGERS SEEN IN DEMOCRATIC CONGREGATIONAL GOVERNMENT

Expansion and trouble went hand-in-hand. With it we soon saw the need to strengthen the organization and readjust its structure in accordance with the arrangement of the early congregation in the days of the apostles. It was becoming more evident that with the growth of the organization, the democratic method of electing "elders" and class "officers" would lead to serious difficulties, besides being out of harmony with Jehovah's way of doing things.

The electing of elders and other officers in the congregations, which was our practice before the present theocratic arrangement was introduced, was a carry-over from the congregational pattern Russell had been used to in his youth. But there were grave dangers present with the system. In many of the religious organizations, such elections were a regular political caucus. Some "sister" would like to have one of her sons or her husband put into a prominent position, and she would make a party for all the "sisters" so that they might come together and have a lovely time. They might discuss a few Scriptures and one thing and another, and then she'd bring up the question in an offhand sort of way: "Who do you think should be elected as elder? Who should be so-and-so, wouldn't my husband—?" and so on.

After Rutherford became president he was not long in seeing that the democratic arrangement was not the proper procedure for the Christian congregation at all. He had been a lawyer and a politician in his youth, and he saw the corruption that was possible in such method. So he turned to the Bible and studied carefully the procedure followed by the disciples of Jesus. What he learned was revealing and certainly ruled out any democratic arrangement if the modern organization was to follow the primitive pattern of the apostles.

THE PRIMITIVE CONGREGATION WAS THEOCRATIC

The original congregation was theocratic. It was ruled by Jehovah God through Jesus Christ. The apostles were selected by Jesus,[2] not elected by the disciples. Every member of the body of Christ was to be set in place by God himself.[3] It was his organization, and he was directing its affairs.

Jesus organized the congregation with various ones performing different responsibilities, so that the entire arrangement would be complete.[4] This didn't mean that the governing body at Jerusalem ruled the others and held their power over them as an arbitrary hierarchy. True, the governing body at Jerusalem were the ones that finally decided certain matters regarding doctrine and practice. As I've mentioned, when the question arose about Paul and Barnabas going to the Gentiles with the message, it caused a furor among the old-fashioned Jews. They said, "No, you can't accept a Gentile into the body of Christ until he first becomes a Jew. He must become circumcised and practice the keeping of the law as the Jews do, then he may be received." Finally the difference became so sharp that Paul and Barnabas went to Jerusalem where an assembly of the governing body was held as recorded in the Fifteenth Chapter of Acts.[5] After considerable debate Peter reminded the assembly that God had sent him to the first Gentile, then Paul and Barnabas told how the Lord blessed their work amongst the Gentiles. James, who was the brother of Jesus and the presiding minister of the Jerusalem congregation, finally summed up the matter that the Gentiles should come in on an equal footing with the rest if they would accept Christ. This decision was based on the written word of the prophets and so recognized as directed by God. It was not an arbitrary decision by the governing body.

As the apostles and others went around preaching the Kingdom message, they did not tell the various groups to elect servants or make elders out of those that were put up for office. The apostles and a few others were authorized by the governing body to appoint men who were already elders, that is, who were mature and well-established in the faith.[6] They were appointed to positions in the various congregations as servants to carry on the work.[7] And this was generally supervised by the governing body at Jerusalem.

Besides taking the lead in the preaching work [8] the governing body was responsible to make reproofs and corrections and direct the conduct of the organization.[9] This could not be done unless those in responsible positions in the congregation were representatives of the governing body, being appointed by it. These appointments were not made by an organization of men, but by the power of God's holy spirit.[10] Hence, those who opposed or resisted the theocratic arrangement were not opposing or resisting men; they were striving against the spirit of God.

THEOCRATIC STRUCTURE RESTORED TO THE CONGREGATION

Now, we argued, if that is the way Jehovah God arranged the congregation in the first place, what authority do we have for a different procedure now? It was recognized too that the Scriptures foretold the theocratic organization would be restored again when the time for Jesus' second presence had arrived.[11] "And he shall send Jesus Christ, which before was preached unto you: whom the heaven must receive until the times of restitution of all things, which God hath spoken by the mouth of all his holy prophets since the world began." These prophets foretold the improved condition that would prevail and the amazing increase that would result: [12] "For brass I will bring gold, and for iron I will bring silver, and for wood brass, and for stones iron: I will also make thy officers peace, and thine exactors righteousness. . . . A little one shall become a thousand, and a small one a strong nation: I the Lord will hasten it in his time."

When these points on organization were cleared up and published in *The Watchtower* in 1938 [13] a further cleansing of the organization was provided. From the days of C. T. Russell there were those who were called "elders," who wore frock coats and black ties; a few spent their time studying and looking up ideas that were not published or printed in the old *Watch Tower*. Their thought was to attract attention to themselves by telling something new, and at times they were doing exactly what Paul warned against in Acts 20:29, 30 where he said, "After my departing shall grievous wolves enter in among you, not sparing the flock. Also of your own selves shall men arise, speaking perverse things, to draw away disciples after them."

When the time arrived for Jehovah to gather together those that would make up his spiritual temple, that was the condition he found, and he proceeded to cleanse the temple from such a group. As I've already told you, he permitted severe trials to come upon the entire Society and the result was that many of these old-time elders were not able to survive and move forward in the expanding service privileges.

Those who refused to swallow their pride and follow the example of Jesus and his disciples in the door-to-door ministry soon found themselves out of the organization entirely. They soon found that all the others of the respective congregations were participating in the witness work which developed them mentally and otherwise brought them along to maturity. These active ones became true "elders" by reason of their loyalty and zeal in the Lord's service. They were not elected to an office of "elder"; but they became elders by their own service activity; then they were appointed to positions of responsibility and service in the organization because they had shown the proper qualifications.[14]

As a result Jehovah's witnesses now prosper under the theocratic arrangement. Without it we never could have had the phenomenal increase we now rejoice in. But all those associated with the Society recognized the necessity for this theocratic arrangement and appreciated the fact that it was laid on the primitive foundation of the apostles. Immediately all the congregations all over the world voted to uphold the arrangement and asked the governing body at the Brooklyn headquarters to appoint those in respective congregations who would serve as overseers. Today there is no confusion and there is no argument about how we proceed or who will have the responsibility for the oversight in each congregation. It is all settled through the theocratic arrangement, exactly as the apostles had it in the days of old. The New World society is being developed and built up and the arrangement that went into effect in 1938 will continue into the new world and for a thousand years of Christ's reign.

THE PRIMITIVE FOUNDATION PROVIDES MATURITY

As in all other features of development, the theocratic structure of the Society was a gradual process. Russell wanted to destroy the pagan idea of the clergy-laity distinction. Rutherford saw that the democratic procedure would inevitably lead to political haranguing. Now we can see it as the Lord's direction. It certainly solves many of our problems. It provides a unity and closeness world-wide that could not be maintained if all congregations acted independently. Besides, continued expansion could not be accomplished with the ease it now is.

Let's say we have a congregation of two hundred ministers, or publishers of the good news. How simple it is to start another congregation. Two groups of one hundred each are divided off into adjoining territories and each group recommends that certain men of their number would be suitable overseers or servants. These names are sent in to the theocratic headquarters and if those recommended meet the rquirements, then the Society may appoint them. True, those who remain at the original location miss the association of those in the other group for a time, but in a little while empty seats are taken by new ones coming in, and the congregation grows up again to be two hundred, and there will be another division. Everything is handled in an orderly way and no serious problems interfere. The same doctrine is taught and the same procedure of operation is carried on in each new congregation.

This theocratic arrangement has carried us through a period of intense opposition. Without the unity of action it has brought us, enabling Jehovah's spirit to move and direct our course, the growing New World society would never have survived to maturity. While this full development in organizational structure did not come until close to twenty years after the New World society had begun to operate, we were still in the midst of severe persecution. In fact, our struggle for survival as a new nation had really only begun.

CHAPTER 12

A SECOND STRUGGLE TO SURVIVE

AFTER THE FIRST ARREST in 1928 for preaching on Sunday we began to encounter a stiffening legal barrier to our work. Objections were based, not on the fact that we were itinerant preachers, but on the message itself that we were proclaiming to the world. As the years progressed this fact became quite obvious in the almost unbelievable variety of laws that were enacted or brought to bear against us.

In most democratic lands, at least, you can't be arrested just because you insist on publicly disagreeing with the powerfully-entrenched major religions of the world. Still, these groups, unable to answer the bold charges made in open discussion and unable to endure the stinging rebuke that was being administered, determined that some means had to be found to put a stop to our work. Pressure was brought to bear on those in public office, as we had experienced in 1918, and many times during those turbulent decades we saw "mischief framed by law." [1] This time, however, I am happy to relate, the federal government of the United States refused to be drawn in.

Perhaps you've heard it said that it is neither brotherly nor neighborly, not even gentlemanly, to speak against another man's religion. Yet those who make this statement overlook the fact that Jesus spent his entire ministry doing it. True, he healed the sick; he raised the dead; he preached [2] "Happy are the merciful, since they will be shown mercy." But he also told leaders of the Jews' religion: [3] "Serpents, offspring of vipers, how are you to flee from the judgment of Gehenna?" Jehovah's earlier prophet, Jeremiah, was divinely commissioned "to root out, and to pull down, . . . to build, and to plant." [4]

Of course, neither Jesus nor Jeremiah was popular with certain groups because they exposed error; but they proved themselves real neighbors—brothers—to the multitudes who were being injured by mistaught ideas of worship. Those people to whom they preached had not realized their way of worship was wrong or injurious. But those who were willing to listen and consider the evidences soon discovered the truth.

I'm sure you'll agree that persecution is not the tool of honest men. None of those who really listened to Jesus persecuted him. Nor is there any record that Jesus and his disciples, or, for that matter, any of the faithful prophets of old ever raised a hand against their adversaries. They exposed false teachings and pronounced God's judgments but never endeavored to stir up the political rulers against their enemies. Both Biblical and secular history show clearly it is only those who advocate false worship who stoop to such means.

Jehovah's witnesses have never resorted to violence or illegal means in defense of their worship. We've been outspoken against those doctrines and religious practices which we do not believe are supported by the Bible but have always relied entirely on the Bible as an offensive weapon, just as the apostle Paul urged us to do.[5]

PIONEERING IN RADIO PREACHING

Another factor had developed besides the Sunday door-to-door work that contributed to the stiffening opposition we were encountering. Not only was Rutherford outspoken, but his idea was to reach as many people as possible. After he clearly saw that this message was a world-wide one, and that it must be proclaimed to all nations of earth, he was endeavoring to find some means whereby this could be done effectively and quickly. Our numbers at that time were so few, he thought our personal house-to-house calls should be augmented. The use of radio was the obvious answer.

Rutherford's first broadcast from a public platform was in 1922, when radio communication was still in its infancy. February 24, 1924, Rutherford inaugurated the Society's own station, WBBR, a pioneer in noncommercial, educational broadcasting, built on Staten Island, New York.

By 1927 radio was really coming into its own. That year the Watch Tower Society used a network of fifty-three stations to broadcast a talk from a convention in Toronto, Canada. Rutherford made full use of it on that occasion and regularly thereafter. One publication on radio personalities of the time spoke of him as an "eloquent Missourian" and accurately reported: [6]

> Judge Rutherford broadcast from Toronto in 1927 at an assembly of fifteen thousand. In 1933 he was heard over five stations in France, and was the first to utilize the largest station in Holland. His hook-up of three hundred sixty-four stations in the United States and Canada established a record for the largest wired network. His stirring words have been heard from coast to coast.

By 1928 we already had a weekly network of thirty stations throughout the United States and Canada, and by 1933 there were 408 radio stations in six continents carrying Rutherford's Bible talks by transcription.

Now the opposition really became bitter. The year 1933 was set aside by our enemies as the year they were going to "drive Rutherford off the air." Extreme pressure was brought to bear against radio station managers by intimidation and threat of boycott. Many yielded and canceled contracts, sometimes right in the middle of a talk. Their excuse was, "Rutherford's talks are too controversial." Has the truth ever been anything else? I remember the 1932 presidential campaign was a hotly contested battle, yet carried by all the big networks. Rutherford paid for every minute of time he used, at commercial rates, and was willing to take full responsibility for all statements he made. This caused many of the more liberal stations to resist intimidation and the campaign to stop Rutherford failed to accomplish its purpose.

SOUND CARS TAKE THE ROAD

At this same time another feature of the work was developed which carried the transcribed lectures to thousands of people. This was the use of sound cars. These automobiles and small panel trucks were equipped with transcription machines and amplifiers connected to loudspeakers on top of the car which broadcast the talks over an extensive area. These cars went out over country roads, in small towns and even in the large cities. They would stop at a point where the most people would be likely to hear and would play recorded Bible lectures. Some of these talks were extremely pointed and often brought an immediate reaction.

One experience I recall was in a Pennsylvania town on the Monongahela River in Fayette County. The town is far down in a hollow and on its east side is a high hill. The town attorney had tried to stop us from preaching with our magazines on the street and to interfere with our service in every possible way. I was appointed to go to see him one Saturday afternoon and discuss the interference with him. I asked him what the reason was for his trying to interfere with our religious work.

"We teach the Bible and nothing but the Bible," I pointed out, "and the United States Constitution backs us up in our religious freedom." I dealt a good deal with the prophecies of the Bible and described our interest in the new way of life, showing him how we were teaching these things.

The old fellow became quite impressed but he said, "I'll tell you what's wrong. The people of this town are very indignant. There are many Catholics here of foreign extraction—they work in the mines. When that loud sound truck of yours got up on the hill and turned on Judge Rutherford's talk, it swept up and down the valley, and stirred the people up to a great extent. They came after us and insisted we had to do something whether it was legal or illegal. It had to be done. Now if you'll just go about it in a different way and in a quiet way, then we'll not interfere with your parades or with your meetings."

It was only a few of the more radical sort that stirred up all the trouble, but they made so much noise by their complaints, the police in many communities became obsessed with the idea that the whole community was against us. That has rarely been true. Except in some strong religious communities we have mostly found the majority of people either willing to listen or just indifferent.

In spite of the widespread use of radio and the extensive door-to-door work that was being done, few people really knew what we believed. Most of the things they heard about us were from our opposers who were making a concerted effort to prejudice the public against us.

ORGANIZING A PEACEABLE COUNTER-ATTACK

Arrests were on the increase and in some communities it was impossible for our people to carry on their work. They would be arrested before they had hardly begun. This called for a bold and decisive campaign. We knew we were authorized from the Bible to preach and we knew that, at least in the United States, the fundamental law of the land guaranteed us that freedom. So we set about to exercise it in a way that would accomplish results and defeat the opposition. We organized a system in the United States that proved successful in covering the territory with the Kingdom message. This is the way it operated.

Volunteers were organized into units that were prepared on any weekend to go to any community within a given radius and preach from door to door. When trouble arose, the one in charge of that particular area would send out a call for as many car groups as would be needed to visit each home in the trouble spot within a space of an hour or so. These volunteer workers would then meet at a designated rendezvous and receive instructions as to which section of the town they were to work, so that before they ever entered the town each minister knew the exact blocks he would be expected to cover. The cars would then drive into town individually and at a set time would start to work. Within the allotted time of one or two hours every home in the city would be visited and the people of the community given a proper chance to hear for themselves the good news of God's kingdom.

In the meantime, at the hour designated for them to begin their house-to-house preaching, two ministers of the delegation would go directly to the police department and report what they were doing. We didn't go in there to ask a permit to do the work. We had that right by virtue of the Constitution and as a God-given commission. We went in there to inform them that we had a number of our Christian workers in the community, presenting the Kingdom message from door to door; and if there were any people calling up, telling them about it, they would know exactly what was going on. Most of the police appreciated this and it prevented arrests in many cases.

These campaigns kept the work going so that the people were being reached even in territories where opposition was intense. But it by no means stopped the arrests. Police as well as other city officials were still misinformed about our work and constant pressure was being applied by the element that had no concern for justice and the rights of others. Our growing organization was still too young and the principles we stand for were not yet recognized by those officials who make and enforce the laws. Gradually, as the facts came out in the open, we began to find their faces more friendly and the honesty of many forced them to recognize our position as entirely within the law and justified. But this did not come in any large measure for a number of years.

ONE JUDGE RENDERS A DECISION

One case that stands out vividly in my mind took place in Honea Path, South Carolina. On that occasion two of our ministers who had been active for a number of years were arrested, and had been in jail for several days. The man who had charge of our divisional campaigns, Anton Koerber, was sent down there to visit the townsfolk, and also to appear in court in behalf of our ministers.

He organized a group of about forty cars, with an average of four people to each, so it represented about 160 workers. On the way down to Honea Path for a radius of about twenty miles they covered all the small towns and isolated houses. When they finally reached the central county courthouse in time for the trial at two o'clock in the afternoon, they found a large number of citizens gathered around outside the building; and as they came on the scene the townsfolk began to mumble and point to them. The Witnesses knew then that these people were waiting for them. Just as the doors were opened and they were about to enter the courthouse, they found that there were two lines of men with clubs and guns, standing at the entrance in a very menacing manner, as much as to say, "We dare you to come in here."

Koerber looked at McLamb, who was the presiding minister of Greensboro, North Carolina, at that time, and one of the captains of the group. "McLamb," he said, "I'm going in there; I have to. I'm scheduled to attend the trial. You had better wait out here so that if anything happens you can get some assistance."

"No," McLamb said, "I'm going in with you; and——"

So in they started, side by side. The crowd lined up before the entrance glowered at them, but did not raise a hand or club against them.

Koerber and McLamb went into the courtroom. The place was packed with townsfolk—our people couldn't even get into the courthouse. No one knew what to expect, but when the trial opened to our surprise and relief the judge permitted an extensive defense, allowing our people to speak freely. He asked a number of questions himself and finally dismissed the defendants with an apology. When they were released and came outside all the inhabitants of the town were waiting for them. Apparently they were as amazed as our people had been because they began to ask questions, and just about took all of the Bible literature that had not been disposed of in the campaign on the way into town.

Those who were there say they will never forget the scene as they returned home just at dusk. As they put their headlights on, one could see the stream of cars, at least a mile or so, and all of Jehovah's witnesses singing songs of thanksgiving and praise for a wonderful day in the Lord's service and for the victory he had given them for holding fast to their worship. That was typical of the joy and the zeal manifested by all those who had part in these divisional campaigns.

THE PHONOGRAPH IS DRAFTED FOR SERVICE

Opposition, however, continued to grow in intensity. Arrests increased, mobbings became more frequent, even contracts with radio stations became more difficult to obtain. Then, in 1937, Rutherford announced Jehovah's witnesses were voluntarily withdrawing from the air. He felt by that time our purpose in using radio had reached its climax, and now a closer contact with the public was being sought. By this time, use of portable phonographs as vehicles for carrying the message had been attempted and found extremely successful. Within a year ninety different four and one-half minute Bible lectures were available in sixteen languages. Our purpose was not to start an argument on some point of doctrine at the homes but to preach the good news of Jehovah's Kingdom in a uniform and efficient way.

Impressing the phonograph into theocratic service had decided advantages over the more impersonal method of reaching the homes through radio loudspeakers. Now we were able to answer questions that arose in the minds of the listeners and a much more effective presentation of our message was accomplished.

Here again, though, a few in the organization failed to recognize their opportunities, refused to pocket their pride and balked at going from door to door with the phonograph. They soon lost interest and now are no longer associated with the organization of Jehovah's witnesses. This served as a further test of our sincerity as to whether we were truly interested in preaching to the world with the most effective means known at the time regardless of how it might effect us personally.

Our voluntary withdrawal from the radio did not bring a halt to the opposition. The phonograph activity was not so conspicuous but it was striking far too deeply and accomplishing far too much good for our opposers to relent in their campaign to suppress us.

A TOTALITARIAN THRUST IS THWARTED

Then, at the height of this bitter fight another element appeared. It gave sure evidence that fascism was making serious inroads into the American way of life. In Detroit, Michigan, a Roman Catholic priest, Charles Coughlin, began to arouse a certain class of persons who formed themselves into groups called "the Christian Front."

In 1939, when Coughlin was feeling his strength, a public address, "Government and Peace," by Judge Rutherford, was widely advertised to be delivered on Sunday afternoon, June 25, in New York's Madison Square Garden. It was to be carried simultaneously by wire and wireless facilities to vast assemblies in numerous cities in this country and other lands. Soon we discovered a concerted effort was being planned to prevent this talk's being given, both in New York and elsewhere. The police were notified days in advance of threats that had been made that the meeting would be broken up, so when the day for the talk arrived they were present in force.

In the course of the actual delivery of the lecture in New York a mob of Coughlin's "Christian Front" men and women, who had planted themselves in the Garden at the last minute, began to boo and shout. Their object was to start a riot and thus break up the meeting. When the interruption actually began, the police made no effort to stop it or assist the staff of Jehovah's witnesses assigned as ushers who attempted to quell the disturbance. Eventually our own ushers had forcibly to eject the troublemakers. Not only did the police refuse to help, but upon insistence of some of the rioters, three of the ushers were arrested and accused of felonious assault. When the case came to trial, however, they were not only exonerated but the three-judge court commended them for their firmness in resisting the attempt to break up the lawful assembly after the police had wholly failed to perform their duty.

Within a few months Coughlin's influence began to wane.

The arrest of a number of men charged with fascist activities who were reportedly associated with his movement brought such notoriety that soon the organization's strength was dissipated.

THE U. S. SUPREME COURT SURRENDERS A FREEDOM

Lack of understanding of our work was aggravated by those who did not wish the people to hear what we had to say. The instigators knew we were not opposed to true Christianity or the Bible, but took the position that since we openly disagreed with their interpretation of the Bible, that made us a threat to organized society. Our position of strict neutrality in world affairs also was misinterpreted and charged against us.

Probably the outstanding example of this was in Germany from 1933 onward. Hitler's rise to power brought extreme persecution to Jehovah's witnesses in that country. There the controversy centered around these Christians' refusal to "Heil Hitler," which was a salute to the authoritarian power. Standing on the grounds of neutrality, Jehovah's witnesses regarded their personal allegiance to any human government as being contrary to the principle stated by Jesus: [7] "Render to Caesar the things that are Caesar's, and to God the things that are God's."

Arbitrary opposition to this stand of Jehovah's witnesses was not confined to Germany. Soon the international nature of a conspiracy to "get" Jehovah's witnesses became quite evident. This same issue was raised in the United States by a few patrioteers and finally came before the Supreme Court in 1940 when Europe was in the first flush of World War II. With but one dissenting vote this high court decided that school boards had the right to choose to require children to salute the American flag.[8] Many Americans who were more sober-minded began to wonder to what extent true democratic principles were being surrendered on the plea of "fighting fascism."

On June 16, 1940, the United States Solicitor General Francis Biddle was moved to state on a coast-to-coast network of NBC:

". . . Jehovah's witnesses have been repeatedly set upon and beaten. They had committed no crime; but the mob adjudged they had, and meted out mob punishment. The Attorney General has ordered an immediate investigation of these outrages.

"The people must be alert and watchful, and above all cool and sane. Since mob violence will make the government's task infinitely more difficult, it will not be tolerated. We shall not defeat the Nazi evil by emulating its methods."

This warning, however, did not prevent opposition. Indeed, that Supreme Court decision of 1940 touched off the most violent wave of persecution yet encountered by Jehovah's witnesses in the United States.

RESPECT FOR GOD GIVEN FIRST PLACE

But why, you might ask, would anyone not want to salute the flag?

It is not that Jehovah's witnesses do not respect the flag or the government that it stands for; it is rather that we have a proper respect for Jehovah God and his Word. We are not trying to convert the world to refuse the salute of a flag. If anyone wants to salute the flag of any nation or enter the armed services of any government that is his right and it would be wrong for anyone, Jehovah's witnesses or anyone else, to oppose him or try to prevent it. However, as the apostle Paul said,[9] "Now then we are ambassadors for Christ." That means Jehovah's witnesses, being dedicated to Jehovah God as his servants, must maintain their position of strict neutrality toward the governments of this world. No worldly ambassador would interfere with the internal affairs of the nation where he is serving the interests of his own country. So we do not. We stay neutral.

Saluting a flag, to Jehovah's witnesses, is to acknowledge salvation as coming from the government the flag represents. Jehovah's witnesses attribute salvation only to Jehovah God and Christ Jesus. So we cannot salute the national emblem of any country without violating God's commandment against idolatry as stated in his Word.[10]

You may have difficulty in appreciating how the simple salute of a respected emblem can amount to idolatry. If you sincerely feel that way we have no argument with you. There are some issues we feel we must preach about to the world. This issue is not one of them. It is strictly an individual matter. We respect the flag for what it represents and try to be as law-abiding as any citizens of a country can be, and will keep all laws of our own countries that do not violate God's supreme law. We do so not because we are afraid of punishment for breaking the law but because it is the right thing to do and the Bible commands us to do what is right. On the other hand, if men make laws contrary to God's law, then we must do as the apostles when they said,[11] "We ought to obey God rather than men."

Even in ancient times men made laws that conflicted with God's laws to his people. One case was on this very point of rendering a salute to an emblem erected as a symbol of the government. Jehovah had commanded his chosen people, the nation of Israel: [12] "Thou shalt have no other gods before me. Thou shalt not make unto thee any graven image, or any likeness of anything that is in heaven above, or that is in the earth beneath, or that is in the water under the earth: Thou shalt not bow down thyself to them, nor serve them."

Would you think that saluting an emblem of a government would be a violation of this law? Well, three of the Hebrew children of God did.[13] When Nebuchadnezzar, king of Babylon, made an image to represent the authority of his state, Shadrach, Meshech and Abednego refused to bow down to it, which was a form of salute. When you realize that these three men were officials of the Babylonian government, you can see what a serious position they put themselves in. Yet their action was approved by God because when they were thrown into the fiery furnace as punishment, Jehovah delivered them unscathed. So the Bible account itself interprets the meaning of God's commandment to us and the position taken by Jehovah's witnesses is not just an arbitrary one. As Paul indicated, we sincerely believe that these things, as examples, "are written for our admonition, upon whom the ends of the world are come." [14] And through this same faithful apostle, God further instructed us, "Wherefore, my dearly beloved, flee from idolatry."

THE INTERNATIONAL NOOSE DRAWS TIGHTER

However, during the heat of patriotic fervor fanned by world conflagration, few persons were willing even to consider why anyone would take such a position. In thousands of communities throughout the land, certain religious elements and "would-be" patriotic elements led men controlled neither by law nor reason to assault thousands of Jehovah's witnesses, men, women and children; destroyed their property; drove them from their homes, burned their houses, places of worship, furniture, books and money; tied groups of them together and forced castor oil in large quantities down their throats; herded them like beasts along hot, dusty roads and railroad rights-of-way in many places, dragged them along the main streets of the city by a rope around their necks and then strung them up; induced public officials to break into homes of private citizens who were Jehovah's witnesses, kidnaped and carried them from one state to another, and broke up their private Bible-study assemblies.[15]

Severe as this opposition was in the United States, it could not compare with what our Christian brothers encountered in

Hitler's Germany and those countries influenced by fascist methods. From 1933 until the end of World War II thousands of Jehovah's witnesses were imprisoned or banished by Hitler while other thousands were forced underground in their preaching activity. As the Nazi juggernaut steamrollered across Europe these same conditions began to prevail in France, Spain, Poland, Belgium, Greece, Bulgaria, Hungary, Italy, the Netherlands, Rumania, Yugoslavia, Estonia, Finland, Denmark and even Norway. In Africa, Northern and Southern Rhodesia, Nigeria and the Gold Coast followed suit. Throughout the British Empire, from Canada to Australia, bans were imposed and in England itself shipment of our literature into the country was prohibited.

As by a giant pincers being applied, our outlying fields of activity were being nipped off one by one and total worldwide proscription seemed imminent. While mob violence in the United States was approaching its peak in 1940, this country still remained isolated from the war and our preaching of the goods news still was free to operate in the open, though seriously hampered by hostile conditions.

Then, December 7, 1941, America was electrified with the blow at Pearl Harbor in a surprise attack.

Immediate entry of the United States into World War II raised serious questions in our minds. How would we fare this time? Would our work at headquarters be violently brought to a standstill again? Or would the closely knit organization under theocratic rule be able to survive? Would our sincere efforts to prove to all men and nations that we were not enemies of the state be recognized? Would we be permitted to provide much-needed comfort and hope to war-ridden and nerve-tattered people of all the nations indiscriminately? Would the position of strict neutrality to which we were dedicated be acceptable and enable us to perform our God-given commission to preach this good news of the Kingdom without serious interference?

Abruptly, for the second time, in the midst of a real crisis

for our movement, the Society lost its president. J. F. Rutherford died January 8, 1942.

FACING THE FUTURE WITHOUT FEAR

C. T. Russell had died when the world was at war, when the
organization of Jehovah's witnesses was still an embryo, when
hostile forces surrounded it, watching for a chance to jump in
and finish it off. The years that followed almost wrecked the
organization. Now history seemed to be repeating itself, bent
on accomplishing an unfinished task.

Again the world was at war, again hostile forces were determined to exterminate the preaching society of Jehovah's
witnesses, again the organization was without a "leader"—but
this time there was a difference. Now we had been rid of creature worship; we had come to recognize Jehovah's dealings,
not with an individual, but with a composite group of fully
dedicated servants; we were fully aware of our proper position
in relation to worldly governments—one of strict neutrality;
we had shaken off the corrupting influence of congregational
rule in favor of theocratic appointment through a central
governing body; we had been brought to a remarkably advanced position in regard to an understanding of Bible doctrine. Would these things make a difference in what lay ahead
of us in the next few eventful years? Or was our work really
finished?

This time we were not afraid. We faced the future confidently. Why shouldn't we? Jehovah, our God, had been
good to us. He had already shown his power of deliverance.
He had showered down on us such blessings that we asked for
nothing more. Yet the events that were still to come, the
manifestation of Jehovah's presence that was still to be revealed, have far surpassed any dreams of the future we might
have had.

PART THREE

THE
NEW WORLD
SURVIVES

CHAPTER 13

THE TRIUMPH OF THE GOOD NEWS

NATHAN HOMER KNORR became the third president of the Watch Tower Bible and Tract Society with hardly a ripple to disrupt the steady operation of our newly established theocratic arrangement.

J. F. Rutherford had been loved and was missed. But he had, himself, worked diligently to tear out the very roots of creature worship or dependency of the organization on individuals. The transition from his presidency in the midst of crucial conditions was a testimony to his success—and Jehovah's blessing on the arrangement.

When news of Rutherford's death came, I was in North Carolina at Elizabeth City, a small place just south of Norfolk, Virginia. That evening a number of us went up to Norfolk since there was no congregation at Elizabeth City, where we were working. At Norfolk the congregation had its regular meeting, and the one presiding that evening made announcement of Rutherford's passing; but beyond that no more was said about it. None said, "What are we going to do now?" or

"How will things go?" Though many individually expressed sorrow to each other after the meeting, they talked generally about other interests of the work and none expressed doubts or fears as to what his passing might mean to the organization.

That was typical of the reaction of all of Jehovah's witnesses. As members of a theocratic organization, we now realized the work would continue as the Lord directed, regardless of whoever might be taking the lead on earth. Rutherford had continually expressed that thought in *The Watchtower;* and by the time he died all associated in the work, including those of the headquarters staff, had become more stabilized and mature in their thinking. Although Rutherford was a vigorous and prominent figure in the organization, yet his somewhat sudden death caused no great upheaval in the work, as it would have if we had been following a man. But Knorr had his work cut out for him from the start.

N. H. Knorr knew the organization inside and out. He had grown up with it—in fact had done much toward its development even while Rutherford was alive. Born April 23, 1905, in Bethlehem, Pennsylvania, he graduated from Allentown, Pennsylvania, High School in 1923 and that same year entered the full-time ministry and became a member of the Bethel headquarters staff. He worked hard and immediately showed his ability at organizing. Martin, who was general manager of the publishing office and plant, took a hand in training him for the work there and when Martin died in 1932 Knorr took his place. Eight years later he was made a director and elected vice-president of the Watch Tower Bible and Tract Society; when, on January 13, 1942, he became president, he was only thirty-six years old. But in the nineteen years he had been at headquarters he had made good use of the time and was well equipped to take on the responsibility of so vast a work. Besides, he had an unshakable faith in Jehovah's theocratic direction of the New World society and a keen desire faithfully to fulfill his own appointment.

With the work seemingly closing down on all sides Knorr's interest was in expanding the preaching. He had no thought of retrenching. He was confident that we had not begun to scratch the surface of the world-wide field that Jesus Christ had said was our preaching assignment. He set out to push the limits of our theocratic boundaries to the ends of the earth, to all lands and to all peoples. No corner was to be left untilled or unplanted.

STABILITY AND STRENGTH DESPITE PERSECUTION

While World War II still raged, Knorr made his first official tour of our branch offices down into Mexico, through the Caribbean area and on into Central and South America. His purpose was to learn first-hand what the conditions of our people were and how they could be helped to advance their activity by sending specially trained missionaries into these fertile fields.

He was accompanied on this tour by Fred W. Franz, vice-president of the Watch Tower Bible and Tract Society, whose facility with the Spanish language made him an invaluable traveling companion. Franz had already shown his value to Knorr in assisting him to discharge his literary responsibilities. A scholar from his youth, Franz is a keen student of the Bible. Born in Covington, Kentucky, in 1893, he carried away the honors of the University of Cincinnati and was offered the privilege of going to Oxford or Cambridge in England under the Rhodes Plan. Instead, in 1914, he entered the full-time ministry. His mother was a devout woman and a sincere Bible student and had brought her children up in that way. When Franz came to headquarters in 1920, Rutherford saw at once that he was a young man of literary ability and possibilities, so he put him to work as an editorial assistant. Besides Spanish, Franz has a fluent knowledge of Portuguese and German and is conversant with French. He is also a scholar of Hebrew and Greek as well as of Syriac and Latin, all of which contribute to making him a thoroughly reliable mainstay on Knorr's editorial staff.

Knorr's trip into Central and South America proved extremely successful. Not only were arrangements made to expand the ministry in those countries where Jehovah's witnesses already were operating, but continued efforts in this area saw new fields opening to these determined "husbandmen of the Lord's vineyard." Then, as soon as the war was over, he headed out for Europe with M. G. Henschel, a director of the Society and administrative aide to the president. The following year Knorr made an extensive trip throughout the Far, Middle and Near East. Again he was accompanied by Henschel, his secretary-companion. In the many lands visited conditions were studied and, as opportunity afforded, missionaries were scheduled and sent out.

The end of the war had brought some immediate relief to imprisoned Witnesses while others were helped as conditions improved in territory now occupied by the Allied forces. It can truly be said that the democratic "earth" had "swallowed up" the totalitarian flood sent out against Jehovah's witnesses,[1] but the victory is God's, not man's. All of our freedoms to preach did not come easily in spite of the democratic conquest of totalitarianism. Constant effort and repeated appeals were required by our local ministers in these countries as well as a persistent battle by our headquarters staff.

What had been the result of totalitarian oppression? Had the voice heralding true freedom for the people been silenced? Had Jehovah's commissioned proclaimers of good news holed-up for the duration, refusing to speak out for fear of dictator-control, withholding the only comforting assurance of release and lasting peace through God's kingdom near at hand?

The record speaks for itself. The stability and strength of our newly-founded theocratic society is manifested in its amazing growth in spite of persecution. In all of Europe Jehovah's witnesses came out of the war three times as numerous as they entered! In Poland alone this increase was six times, and within five years after the war they had grown to eighteen times their number! Released from the ban, after three years, Canadian Witnesses came above ground to find four thousand more ministers added to their former six thousand; while in Australia, after only two years, one thousand more had joined the 2,800. Just so, continued growth was evident in all parts of the globe.

A SUCCESSFUL CAMPAIGN ON THE HOME FRONT

While Knorr was developing the expansion in foreign fields, he was still mindful of the bitter battle being waged against us in the United States. When he became president the fight was at its height and getting more intense. The battle for freedom of speech and worship in the United States Supreme Court had already won for Jehovah's witnesses under the able lawyership of H. C. Covington a number of significant victories, but Knorr did not stop here. He knew that our enemies were still determined to finish us as an organization by any means they could command. Deliberate lies about us were being told to people who relied on their informers for the truth. In America we were accused of being Nazis and Fascists, while all the time our Christian brothers in Germany and Italy and other Axis countries were being thrown into prison as American agents and sympathizers. This patriotic passion, fired by World War II, was at white heat.

Then in 1943, when Covington, a director and legal counselor for the Society, presented a new flag case to the highest court of the United States of America, the Supreme Court reversed its judgment on the flag-salute issue,[2] ruling that conscientiously-objecting children have a constitutional right to refrain from saluting a flag. In denying school boards the right to expel children from school for refusal to give the required salute to the flag, the court said: "If there is any fixed star in our constitutional constellation, it is that no official, high or petty, can prescribe what shall be orthodox in politics, nationalism, religion, or other matters of opinion or force citizens to confess by word or act their faith therein."

The legal war on the home front in this country continued to be fought out in the courts of the land. Issue after issue, every legal barrier thrown up by the enemy was exposed and legally knocked out. Victory after victory was chalked up until, by the middle of 1955, over forty favorable decisions in the United States Supreme Court had buttressed our strong constitutional position.

THE FEDERAL GOVERNMENT'S LIBERAL VIEW

During this struggle Knorr refused to compromise the principles of the Society in regard to our stand of neutrality. This firm position, misunderstood as it was by the general public and misrepresented as it was by our avowed enemies in clerical and "patriotic" circles, still was recognized and respected by the Federal Government. Throughout the entire period of World War II we were not disturbed on this government level. I was talking to our legal counsel, Hayden C. Covington, about this the other day, and his comments were interesting and revealing.

"Hayden," I asked, "why is it that, since the Espionage Law is still on the books, the Government didn't try to prosecute us during World War II as they did in 1918?"

"The main reason why is because we weren't guilty and the Government knew it," he answered. "Had Jehovah's witnesses or any of the officers of the Society been guilty of illegal action under the Espionage Law, they would have been prosecuted during World War II under the same act. Failure of the Government to take action under the Espionage Law in World War II proves that none were guilty."

"Hasn't the Government's attitude changed somewhat about prosecutions under this law?"

"Yes. It's now recognized that conscientious objection to participation in the armed forces and explanations of the reasons of such objections to the public are not a violation of the Espionage Act. During the early part of World War II a number of favorable decisions were rendered by the Supreme Court of the United States concerning the validity of the work of Jehovah's witnesses and the non-seditious character of their literature. These decisions buttressed Jehovah's witnesses against a prosecution under the Espionage Law and the Department of Justice knew that."

"Don't you think the Government was more liberal during World War II?"

"Yes, I do. The attitude of the Federal Government during World War II was much more liberal than during World War I."

"Why do you suppose that was?"

"I'll tell you the reason. It's that a number of court decisions in favor of freedom of speech were rendered after World War I and before World War II. These caused the Department of Justice to change its old reactionary attitude for limitation of freedom of speech of conscientious objectors.

"It's commendable that the Department of Justice was more liberal and less susceptible to war hysteria under the Administration of President Roosevelt than it was under the Administration of President Wilson. President Roosevelt and his Attorney General, Francis Biddle, were highly in favor of allowing the maximum amount of freedom of speech in the United States, even while the war was being prosecuted. The very fact that Congress itself provided for the exemption from military service of persons having religious objection to participation in the war also helped to make the attitude of the Department of Justice liberal."

"What, then, would you say was the reason we had so much trouble over the draft in World War II?"

"Most of our trouble resulted from the attitude taken by some local boards and District Courts. A small proportion of the draft boards during World War II were extremely fair. At first great prejudice was shown by many federal District judges. But after the large number of cases continued to flow through their courts many of the judges began to change and mellow. They afterward took a more restrained attitude in presiding at the trial of cases involving Jehovah's witnesses.

"The National Headquarters of the Selective Service System, acting through General Hershey, was also fair. Arrangements were made between him and me for the exemption of our full-time ministers and members of the Bethel Family. He wrote an opinion for guidance of boards on this policy. Some draft boards obeyed this but others did not. It was the arbitrary and capricious determinations that were made by these boards denying the ministerial and conscientious-objector claims for exemption that resulted in prosecutions against Jehovah's witnesses for violating the draft law.

"Approximately 4,500 of Jehovah's witnesses were sentenced to prison in the District Courts because they were denied the right to show that draft boards had violated the law in denying the ministerial or conscientious-objector claims. This practice was approved by the Supreme Court in the *Falbo* [3] decision rendered during the war. But after the war in Europe was over a change came. Then the court decided the *Estep* [4] case in our favor, reversing and condemning the practice of denying Jehovah's witnesses their rights to defend against the indictments brought against them.

"The attitude of the District judges, with exception of one or two throughout the entire United States, was totally antagonistic. They were against any defense being made by Jehovah's witnesses at their trials. This attitude, of course, changed when the Supreme Court decided the *Estep* case. But this was too late to help the 4,500 men who had gone to prison without a right to be heard."

COVERING A CIRCUIT OF TWENTY PRISONS

These 4,500 men presented a problem in the Federal prisons. Not that they were unruly. On the contrary. But prison officials as well as our Society had an interest in their spiritual welfare, and there were no prison chaplains in a position to give our boys the sort of Scriptural counsel they were seeking. Arrangements were finally made with Mr. James V. Bennett, Director of the Federal Bureau of Prisons, for T. J. Sullivan and me to visit the prisons regularly to preach to our boys, comfort them and give counsel on the various Bible study meetings they were conducting among themselves as well as to help them and their wardens on any problems that might arise between them. In addition, arrangements were made for the Society's literature to be mailed into the prisons.

I was assigned to visit about twenty of these institutions once every six weeks. To make the circuit I traveled thirteen thousand miles. Trains were crowded everywhere with soldiers and their families being moved from place to place. I spent many nights in smoking-cars that made me feel like a smoked ham next day. I spent many hours in small stations at junction points waiting for late trains. It was strenuous business traveling those days but the joys of my assignment compensated me.

One of the more serious problems I had to deal with, as I remember, was vaccinations. An order was received from the health department in Washington for all the inmates and guards to be vaccinated. Some of our boys in one prison in particular considered this the same as blood transfusions, and refused to submit. This caused considerable trouble. Then the order came from Washington to put all the men who refused to be vaccinated in solitary confinement. This did not change our men. The prison authorities hesitated to be overly strict about it; still they had their orders from headquarters. Well, during the excitement I arrived on my regular visit. Now the matter was put up to me to advise our men.

I asked the Warden to permit me to talk to all the men who refused to be vaccinated.

He said, "We can't do that because all the men are in solitary on orders from Washington and they'll have to stay there until they submit."

"Well," I answered, "they'll be there all their lives, then, for they're not the kind to go contrary to their consciences. Now if you'll permit me to talk to all the men we can do something, but with some in solitary I'm helpless."

Then the Warden phoned Washington and told them what I said. He was told to permit all the men to attend the meeting and to allow them to spend as much time in the meeting as Macmillan thought best.

We had an interesting time. For about half an hour the men talked about the evils of vaccination, and so on. After all had had their say, I told them, "We're wasting time talking about the evils of vaccination because much could be said both ways. The point for us to consider is what are we going to do about being vaccinated. They have you all where they could vaccinate an elephant, and they will vaccinate you all."

Up spoke the leader of the resistance and said: "What would you do if you were in prison and were called up for vaccination?"

"I was in prison," I reminded them, "and I bared my arm and received the shot. Furthermore, all of us who visit our foreign branches are vaccinated or we stay at home. Now vaccination is not anything like blood transfusion. No blood is used in the vaccine. It is a serum. So you would not be violating those Scriptures which forbid taking blood into your system.[5]

"You might think the vaccine would pollute the blood stream and that you should refuse on those grounds. Remember the account of what happened to Paul when he was shipwrecked.[6] He went with others to gather wood to keep a fire burning to warm them and a deadly viper attached itself to his hand. The heathen natives of the Island thought Paul might be a murderer who, since he had escaped death in the sea, was to be punished by death from that viper's bite. However, Paul shook the viper from his hand into the fire and suffered no harm.

"Now why don't you act as the prophet Jeremiah did when the princes were urged by the clergymen to try him and have him put to death? He said: [7] 'I am in your hands, now do with me as you wish, but know if you put me to death you will bring innocent blood on yourselves and this city, for Jehovah sent me to tell you all these words.' At that the Princes told Jeremiah that they did not think he was worthy of death."

HEEDING SCRIPTURAL COUNSEL

Our discussion lasted about two hours, then the men decided to submit to vaccination after making a token resistance. Furthermore they agreed to write a letter of apology for the trouble they had caused through their first stand taken.

It was now about 10 P.M. I went down to the Warden's office where the prison doctor and Warden were waiting. They wanted to know how I had got along with the men. I asked them, "If the men submit to vaccination, will any of their privileges or good time be taken away from them for their refusal in the first place?"

The Warden answered, "No, all will be forgotten if they do as you say. We like your men and believe they're sincere, and don't like the idea of punishing them for refusing to do what they think is wrong." To this the doctor agreed.

"But what I'd like to know," the warden continued, "is how did you get the men to agree to being vaccinated?"

"Well, I simply showed them their responsibility and pointed out that if evil resulted the government would be held responsible."

"We told them that, too, but it didn't convince them."

"The difference was, I talked the Bible to them, and that Book Jehovah's witnesses obey."

"Yes, I'm beginning to believe that," was the Warden's conclusion.

The attitude of this warden was quite generally manifested throughout the entire penal system. The Bureau of Prisons and the wardens in the various institutions cooperated in every way and all deeply appreciated the good relationship we were able to establish. Early in the war all misunderstandings were cleared up and from then on everything went smoothly. In fact, many of our boys incarcerated in prison made lasting friendships with officers under whom they served. I know I have in my own possession a letter, which I value highly, written to me by Mr. Bennett. The concluding paragraph states:

"I write this note just to thank you for understanding our position and aiding your men to understand it also. This is not the first time that you have helped us with some of the perplexing problems with which we have been confronted. I most earnestly hope that whenever you are in Washington you will drop in to see me. You will be cordially welcome at any time."

OVERCOMING THE WORLD

The memory of these 4,500 young men imprisoned for their faith often stirs my mind. Talking to them as I did, discussing their personal and collective problems, my faith was immeasurably strengthened. Have you considered what it costs a man to voluntarily submit to a penitentiary sentence for his conscience's sake? I knew what those boys were up against, for I had been in the same condition. Yet when I thought of our Christian brothers in the concentration camps of Europe, as these boys also did, our load seemed lighter.

Paul, the apostle, admonished us: [8] "Consider him who endured from sinners such hostility against himself, so that you may not grow weary or faint-hearted. In your struggle against sin you have not yet resisted to the point of shedding your blood."

The perfect example for all whose Christian fortitude is being tested to the limit is Jesus Christ. He died for us, yet through his death provided release. "In the world you have tribulation; but be of good cheer, I have overcome the world." [9] Is not that victory worth any price we must pay to attain it?

CHAPTER 14

EXPANDING THE EDUCATION
FOR LIFE

EVEN BEFORE World War II came to an end, in fact while the work was closing down on all sides, N. H. Knorr turned his attention to providing even further strength to the organization with the thought of expansion. He began with the individual minister.

Knorr knew that the organization could be no stronger than the individuals who compose it. He knew the New World society could accomplish no more than its associated ministers were qualified to do. He knew that if each one of Jehovah's witnesses were to fulfill his own personal vow of dedication to Jehovah he must individually be trained and equipped. (See Luke 12:47.) After he became president he wasted no time in setting in motion what has probably become one of the most extensive educational campaigns ever conducted. This is the way it came about.

KNORR ORGANIZES FOR EXPANSION

Knorr's close association with Rutherford in his last days enabled him to know precisely what he had in his mind concerning the operation of the organization. Of course, he had thoughts too where the work could be expanded; so when the theocratic organization began to operate in 1938, even before he became president, Knorr saw the need of training those in the organization to handle their work efficiently and to coordinate all efforts for expansion of the work. He encouraged and succeeded in setting in motion an arrangement whereby all countries would be divided into zones, each zone composed of twenty congregations. A zone servant was appointed to visit the congregations in his zone. In addition assemblies were arranged for all the congregations in a zone. Rutherford recognized the benefits such an arrangement could bring, and on October 1, 1938, set it in operation.

Within three years the number of active ministers in the field had more than doubled. However, Rutherford felt the work had accomplished its purpose by that time, and it was discontinued December 1, 1941. In a special letter issued to all congregations he encouraged all of Jehovah's witnesses to stand on their own feet and maintain their ministry, come what may. This certainly seemed like needed counsel because, within a few days after his letter was circulated throughout the United States, this country was involved in World War II, and only a little more than a month later Rutherford himself was dead.

Knorr realized much work lay ahead and that many more people were yet to see the need to dedicate their lives to Jehovah God and serve him before the full end was to come at Armageddon. Because of the severe trials coming on Jehovah's witnesses, they would need further counsel and training, especially new ones associating with the work. So in the fall of 1942, his first year as president, he reorganized the zones into circuits and set in motion a revised arrangement of the work. Four years later, he further revised the work and again arranged for assemblies to be held twice a year in each circuit. Again expansion came rapidly.

PERSONAL MINISTRY RECEIVES ATTENTION

Organizationally we were now on solid footing, and the maturity of the Society as a whole was quite evident. But Knorr realized that every minister must be personally equipped to preach. Rutherford had brought unity to the work by carrying the one message to the public through his radio talks, transcriptions and phonograph recordings. Now Knorr embarked on a campaign to bring maturity to every one of Jehovah's witnesses and especially prepare them to preach individually yet without contradicting one another.

Have you ever noticed how different ministers, representing the same religious organization, teach somewhat different ideas on the same subject? Conferences within their church systems are continually trying to iron out these differences, yet they persist. Knorr believed that not only should all Christians be ministers, but all should teach in exact unity of thought. Would this be possible without making "parrots" of them? Knorr believed it could be, and set out to do it.

About forty or fifty years ago we had many associated with the work who were well-informed as far as the doctrines of the Bible were concerned; but to get a few men to go out and give lectures to congregational meetings or to the public, even in small halls, was a task. It would have been difficult to get as many as thirty or forty to do that. Well now, as far back as 1902 we saw the necessity of training, but our efforts along that line were limited. I was out in Kansas City where we had a home for our full-time workers or "colporteurs." There were five of us who knew little of the art of public speaking, so we established what we called the School of the Prophets, the object being that we would meet certain nights of the week and each one would be allowed ten minutes' talking. We used a chart depicting the ages of man's history in God's purposes and talked from that, and the others would counsel or criticize him. It was mostly criticism and some of it would certainly sound strange to us today. Of course, speaking from the public platform in the early part of this century was totally different from what it is now.

Still, much improvement was made since then in a general way in our ability to present matters from the public platform. In fact, a number of those in the organization were recognized as accomplished speakers. But Knorr wanted everyone in the organization to be "ready always to give an answer to every man that asketh you a reason of the hope that is in you." [1]

INDIVIDUAL TRAINING BRINGS MATURITY

Now the training program began in earnest. In April of 1943 special schools were organized in every congregation of Jehovah's witnesses which became a regular part of congregational activity. These schools provided for an intensified course in public Bible speaking. All male persons attending the meetings were invited to enroll, since training was to be voluntary, and most did. Each week an instruction talk on some feature of public speaking, composition, grammar and related subjects was considered and, later, the Bible itself was discussed from every aspect. Then three student talks were given by those enrolled, each taking his turn. They spoke on assigned Bible topics and then were given counsel for improvement by the one in charge of the school.

These schools, called Theocratic Ministry Schools, are still a vital part of the program of each congregation, and as new male persons become associated they are encouraged to participate. Since the continuous course began, the entire Bible has been summarized through talks given by students. It has also been read through, as well as its outstanding doctrines discussed.

No one graduates. They keep on giving student talks and keep on working for improvement—many, like me, having been enrolled since the schools started. Is it any wonder that now there are associated with Jehovah's witnesses literally thousands who are seasoned speakers from the public platform? Many of these speak regularly at our conventions before hundreds and thousands of people. So it is that individual preaching finally began to come into its own in 1943.

Two years after our Theocratic Ministry Schools had been started we began an extensive public meeting campaign. Our purpose was to preach to all the world that Jehovah's kingdom under Christ had begun, and now that qualified public speakers were being developed in the organization we began to use them.

Everyone had a part. It was not just a matter of someone's preparing and delivering an hour's lecture to an audience. An extensive campaign of house-to-house advertising was conducted in the neighborhood of each talk. Interested persons were given personal invitations and in many instances those lacking transportation would be picked up and taken to the hall. All of those associated with the congregations shared in this advertising work. Saturday afternoons handbills were distributed at busy intersections as well.

As a result of this work more people became acquainted with the message of Jehovah's witnesses and many who are now actively engaging in the ministry themselves had their first contact with the organization at one of these public Bible lectures.

GILEAD SCHOOL SPEARHEADS THE GLOBAL FRONT

Our schools of advanced ministerial training and the public meetings organized in the congregations were really like an extension of something else that had previously been set in motion to expand the training to the ends of the earth.

Much work had been done in the United States beginning back in the 1880's, and it had expanded to most of the major countries of the world as we have seen. But in many places where there were none of Jehovah's witnesses—or very few, as in Africa, Italy, Japan and so on; there was considerable need to organize the work in a theocratic way. Knorr found the solution in the Watchtower Bible School of Gilead.

The school was established on a seven-hundred-acre farm of the Society in the beautiful "Finger Lakes" region of upper New York State, about 250 miles from the Brooklyn headquarters. A rigid curriculum was provided in a wide variety of subjects, particularly suited to prepare these young ministers for the advanced field of foreign missionary activity. In 1943 the first class of one hundred students graduated from the school and was ready to go to foreign lands for an indefinite stay as missionaries. Their new assignment was to be their new home. That was the agreement they made when they volunteered to accept whatever location Knorr selected for them, according to the needs of the field.

It was planned that two groups of approximately one hundred students each be given the complete course each year, and by 1955 those enrolled had been drawn from forty-five countries, trained and sent out to one hundred lands. Over 1,800 are now happy in their assignments and busy preaching.

Missionaries of Jehovah's witnesses don't carry on their work the same way other missions do. In these out-of-the-way places they carry the good news right to the homes of the people, no matter if they have to go back into the bush of the native jungles to do it. It means learning the language of the people and respecting their customs, although in their own missionary homes they are free to maintain American or European standards as much as is practicable. Many cases are reported where those who were illiterate have been taught to read the Bible for themselves so they might become proficient in the true doctrine.

Some missionary societies obtain converts by setting up establishments for feeding and clothing the natives, but I think you'll readily agree a full stomach doesn't necessarily make a man a Christian. Jehovah's witnesses, on the other hand, have endeavored to teach these people how to live by God's standards, to clean up their lives and their homes, and they show them what is required of those who will share in the New World after Armageddon. Those who dedicate themselves to God with this kind of understanding are not easily shaken from their faith and their new course of life makes them more highly respected in their community as clean-living people. Invariably this changed outlook enables them to improve their own living standards, and they learn to stand on their own feet and not depend on some foreign society for continued handouts.

The objective of Jehovah's witnesses in these countries as in all our activity is not to get a large following, but to have only persons of genuine faith in God and Christ associate with our organization. If you're taught the pure Bible truth and encouraged to claim Christianity because of true belief and not for personal gain, you'll endure even under great persecution or trouble and will hold to your faith. The history of those associated with the Society is proof of this. That's pleasing to God. We believe in God and want to do what is pleasing to him.

SCHOOLING THE UNLEARNED TO READ

A few years ago a niece of mine graduated from the Watchtower Bible School of Gilead and went to Chile with other missionaries. That was in December, 1949. At that time there were only around two hundred of Jehovah's witnesses in the whole country. Now there are over 1,100.

An experience she wrote me of some time ago demonstrates the response to their work and the general attitude of the people there.

She was in the bank one day cashing a check from the Society to cover her expenses. Waiting in line was a native clergyman. When she got up to the window the priest said to her, "I see you have a check from New York. Are you an American?"

"Yes, I am," she answered.

"Well, what are you doing down here, just visiting?"

"No," she said, "I'm a missionary."

"A missionary? Don't you know who I am?"

"Yes, I judge by your attire that you are a clergyman."

"Don't you think we will take care of the spiritual needs of the people here?"

"Well sir, it's hard to figure why it is that we have to come down from New York to teach your people how to read what's in the Bible. Why don't you do it?"

Then the cashier spoke up, "Yes, Father John, I wondered about that myself."

My niece reports that ended the conversation.

Chile is just one of the countries in South America that has had such surprising success. Seeing this growing interest in Bible education on the part of the people of the world is gratifying indeed, so I am always a little amused when I read what some writers have to say about it. For instance, *Our Sunday Visitor* recently stated,[2] "The masses of newly transplanted Puerto Ricans of New York and the Mexicans of California and the Southwest have contributed substantial numbers to the sect's membership. Indeed, the organization is making some of its most sizable gains in backward countries where illiteracy abounds." Yet some of those countries where these "gains" are being made are those where this writer's own religion has controlled the education of the people for centuries.

But what of Europe? Would you think this was a field for missionaries? Probably many Europeans wouldn't. During the war years, as I've already mentioned, the work tripled, but since 1942—the year before any graduates of Gilead were sent out by the Society—the work has increased ten times! This shows expansion is not the result of persecution. In 1942 there were 22,896 preaching Witnesses. In 1955 there were 227,374. That means that in a little over a dozen years each witness of Jehovah has become ten in Europe. Doesn't that sound like the prophecy in Zechariah that says: [3] "In those days it shall come to pass, that ten men shall take hold out of all languages of the nations, even shall take hold of the skirt of him that is a Jew, saying, We will go with you: for we have heard that God is with you."

NO DOCTRINAL MATCH FOR THE NOVICE WITNESS

There are millions of people in the world today who are in the same mental attitude I was when I found the faith that has carried me through more than half a century. They realize there is much about God and the Bible that they should know and would like to know, but which they have not been taught although many have attended their church for years. If you are one of these then think seriously on the things I have been telling you. There will be many who will try to discourage you. I have met some but I have always tried to find out the facts. Those who do not have the truth cannot argue against it. If they are opposed to the truth for some reason of their own, then they will try to counteract it by telling things that are not true. But the truth cannot be hidden for long if you are really interested in finding it. Jesus said: [4] "Ye shall know the truth, and the truth shall make you free."

You may be told you can't understand the Bible, that you are too young or too old or not educated enough or that it is a mystery intended for only a select few who spend their entire lives at it as "specialists" in the field. But in the days of the nation of Israel Jehovah God commanded that everyone assemble to hear the Law read, even the babes in arms,[5] and instructed the parents that they were to teach their children in their own homes.[6] That means even those who were not priests were qualified to talk about God's Word. You will remember, too, that Jesus said,[7] "Suffer little children, and forbid them not, to come unto me for of such is the kingdom of heaven." The apostles Peter and John were trained by Jesus, yet were looked down upon as "unlearned and ignorant men." [8]

Jehovah's witnesses make a thorough study of the Bible, which equips them far beyond any natural abilities they might have. This requires those who are opposing our work to try to prejudice inquiring persons away from the message we are preaching. An interesting instance of this appeared recently in *Our Sunday Visitor*.[9] It carried a series of articles on Jehovah's witnesses with the usual misrepresentations of the personalities of Russell, Rutherford and Knorr. If the name and truth of Jehovah God were not involved, many of the statements would be laughable to me. I've lived through most of the entire history of the Society and I've seen these things first-hand. Furthermore, sufficient factual evidence is available to show anyone really seeking information the truth of the matter. But the real significance of the series to my mind was contained in a letter that appeared in the publication a few weeks later.

The letter was addressed to John A. O'Brien, author of the

series. It read: [10] "This is to thank you for the splendid articles on Jehovah's Witnesses in O.S.V. They are factual and irrefragable. Last night a young matron of the parish came into the office, all confused by the literature of the Witnesses. She had begun by trying to convert them and—poor thing—with only a grade-school education, she fell before their glib tongues. At first I tried meeting her objections head on and got nowhere. Finally I pulled out the current issue of O.S.V. and read your article to her. That did it. The discussion was closed. 'If their founder was a rascal like that,' she said, 'I'm through with them.' Yours the credit, yours the merit! Rev. Richard Ginder."

The writer of this letter probably hasn't realized he is admitting that when it came to a discussion of the straightforward doctrine of the Bible, even with his years of college and seminary training, he was no match for this woman "with only a grade school education," who had studied with Jehovah's witnesses for only a short time. He had to resort to "name calling" and had a ready tool at hand provided by O'Brien. That's an easy way to argue, isn't it?—if you can get away with it! But even Jesus was called a man who had a "devil," "gluttonous, and a winebibber." [11] And he said they would treat his true followers the same way.[12]

Evidences are mounting every day and every year that not all people are as easily deceived as it is claimed this woman was. The records show that Jehovah's witnesses are increasing in number by leaps and bounds. Not just in "paying members" like so many of the modern revivalists seek, but in live, active preaching ministers who give freely of their time and strength to carry forward the good news of God's kingdom. Not only do these individuals become acquainted with the Word of God themselves but they also become qualified to teach others the things they have learned.

Jesus told Peter that if he would show his love for Christ, then he must feed God's "sheep." [13] How can a man help someone else to Christianity until he is stabilized and mature himself as a Christian? If he constantly depends on a "pastor" himself for food then he will never be able to demonstrate his own love for Jesus by feeding God's "sheep."

DOORSTEP PREACHING LOCATES THE "SHEEP"

All of the personal training and individual assistance that Knorr has inaugurated has played an important part in the expansion program, and the individual minister using the door-step as his pulpit has really located the sheep of the Lord. If people of the world are to be instructed in God's will for them, it isn't just a matter of learning the Golden Rule and how to live by it or sitting in a building listening to one man preach. It is really a matter of trained men and women going to the people from house to house.[14]

Today, if you want to be a mature Christian you must be a minister or servant of Jehovah, for maturity means not only being acquainted with the fundamental doctrines of the Bible but becoming mature in practicing the truths in his Word. As a Christian, then, you must develop in maturity in the study of God's Word, understanding what is written in his Word and applying it in your life, helping those not yet brought to this deeper understanding of God's requirements to do the same thing.[15]

Ministers should be able to preach, and the special training program being carried on in all congregations of Jehovah's witnesses has equipped them to do that. Now Jehovah's witnesses who call at your door are prepared to give short sermons on a variety of subjects depending on the circumstances and the time you have to listen. The Scriptures are read from the Bible so that we have a common ground for a discussion, and even if you don't accept the Bible as God's inspired Word, at least it gives a recognized foundation for considering current world problems. It will be worth your while to listen carefully to the next one of Jehovah's witnesses who comes to your door.

Today, there is really no distinction of clergy and laity in the organization of Jehovah's witnesses. This is a society of ministers, each with his own pulpit, the doorsteps of the people. Those who appreciate that there is always something to be gained by an honest and friendly discussion of the Bible listen to us at the doors and, while some do not agree with us, in recent years we often hear the expression, "I think you are doing a good work anyway."

What a change in a few years! But it has been persistent walking and talking that has accomplished it. Determined preaching in the face of real adversity, faith in the conviction the people must be warned of Armageddon's approach and comforted with the hope of a New World of righteousness at hand. Don't you think an increase in the last ten years of 350 percent in those now preaching in 160 lands indicates how reasonable it is to believe?

But such an extensive operation as this costs money. Have you been wondering how Jehovah's witnesses are financed? Many persons do. Before I finish my story I'd like to tell you something about that.

CHAPTER 15

JEHOVAH PROVIDES FOR HIS FAMILY

"SEATS FREE, no collection" is a slogan that Jehovah's witnesses are glad to use. We know of no other organization that has operated on any large scale with absolutely no solicitation or collection. Yet from its small beginning in Allegheny, Pennsylvania, in 1872, the Society has reached its present world-wide extent, owning property worth millions of dollars paid for and maintained completely by voluntary contributions.

This policy of operation was stated by Jesus in sending out his twelve apostles to preach: [1] "Freely ye have received, freely give." This text is often quoted during the "offertory" service at churches, but it was not money Jesus was asking them to give when he said that. It was works of service in the ministry they were to give. Read the entire chapter and note what he said. Then he told them not to worry about their financial return because he promised: [2] "The workman is worthy of his meat."

It was in line with this commandment of Jesus to give freely that C. T. Russell published in the second issue of the *Watch Tower* magazine: " 'Zion's Watch Tower' has, we believe, JEHOVAH for its backer, and while this is the case it will never *beg* nor *petition* men for support. When He who says: 'All the gold and silver of the mountains are mine,' fails to provide necessary funds, we will understand it to be time to suspend publication."

That was published in August of 1879 and today, without ever having missed an issue since it started, three million copies are printed each issue.

C. T. Russell used his own personal fortune at the outset, which helped give the work a good start. Rutherford financed many of his preaching trips out of personal savings accumulated before he became associated with the Society. And today, much of the money that is used to carry on the work is spent out of the pocket of the individual minister of Jehovah's witnesses as he engages in the work himself.

VOLUNTARY CONTRIBUTIONS PAY IT ALL

You may never have realized it, but when Jehovah's witnesses come to your homes and knock on your doors it is costing them money. They pay their own carfare or automobile expense and the cost of any literature they give away. They pay the printing cost of books they receive from the Society and contributions they receive for them are used to obtain more. If they give literature away, this money is out of their own pocket. Do you have any idea how much is contributed to the work in this way?

It is nothing for one of the witnesses in most countries to spend two dollars in a month for travel expenses carrying on his ministerial activity. Multiply that by six hundred thousand ministers throughout the world and you can see what it amounts to. Millions of dollars every year are spent by Jehovah's witnesses personally just to visit you and your neighbors in your homes.

In addition to their own individual ministry, each one contributes voluntarily to support the local congregation's expenses, such as rent, electric light, heating and so on. At none of these meetings is a collection ever taken. Boxes are provided at the rear of the hall for anyone who wishes to make a voluntary contribution. No one knows who gives, or how much.

But what about the other features of the work? Building and operating large printing plants, shipping millions of pieces of literature all over the world, maintaining hundreds of missionary homes in over one hundred countries—that all costs money. Where do Jehovah's witnesses get the financial support for all of this activity?

One thing you can be sure of. The contributions we receive for literature at the doors wouldn't begin to pay for it all. In the first place, the amount of contribution is figured to cover little more than printing cost. Then, besides that, much of the literature is given to full-time ministers at considerably below printing cost to help them defray their own distribution expenses. So money for these other features of the work must come from another source—and it does.

For many years now the Society has put a notice in *The Watchtower* once a year requesting each one who wishes to contribute during the year to state how much he wants to contribute and how the contributions would be sent, whether all at once or a certain amount at a time. The reason this has been done is in order that we might know how to lay out the work for the year to come; and the work is planned or expanded on the basis of what is indicated by these expressions. This would indicate the leading of the Lord in spreading the work.

These statements of their good hopes Jehovah's witnesses have never considered as promises or pledges, just simply what they hoped to be able to contribute toward the spreading of the work the coming year. Sometimes some would fall down

on them while others would double up what they had anticipated giving. New ones would come in to the organization and
many contributions would be made by those who did not send
in any expression of their hopes. This has proved very satis-
factory in arranging the year's work, and does not constitute
in any way a solicitation because no one is asked to give a
penny. Neither is an amount established as a goal to be at-
tained. The work progresses only to the extent of the voluntary contributions. That means those entrusted with spending
this money have a real responsibility, and all three presidents
of the Society have been extremely careful not to spend it for
things that would not bring some advancement to the work.
Yet when it is necessary they will spend thousands of dollars
for equipment and millions for new buildings to expand the
preaching program. In doing all this, Jehovah's witnesses have
always managed to pay as they go.

"THE PEOPLE BRING MORE THAN ENOUGH"

There is an interesting story in that connection I'd like to tell
you. It has to do with building our first factory at 117 Adams
Street in Brooklyn.

After the work was revived in 1919 our expansion was so
rapid we outgrew one place after another and finally the question arose about building a real plant of our own that would
meet all of our requirements. Plans were drawn up and we
concluded that it would require an eight- or nine-story building. This was in 1926.

It was going to cost a substantial sum of money, so Martin,
the factory manager, and I got together and talked it over. We
went to Rutherford and said, "Brother Rutherford, if you
would issue notes at a reasonable interest and offer them to our

own people you'll get all that is necessary to build the factory and it would be in the family."

"Oh," he said, "if I set out something like that in *The Watch Tower*, that would cause a furor, it would disrupt the organization. They'd say, Look at them now, they've started in begging."

"But you wouldn't be soliciting or asking for contributions. Just a loan. Why don't you do this? Put a little supplement in there, not as a regular part of the *Tower*. Tell the friends all about it, what the money's for and how it will be used, and I'll guarantee you that in no time at all there will be sufficient funds to build that factory, because everybody in the truth that's devoted to Jehovah is as interested in it as we are and I think it will thrill them to think they can have some part in it."

Well, Rutherford didn't say much after that but he became quite serious and thought about it. Sure enough, he did issue that special edition of the *Watch Tower* and sent it out.

I left on a trip about that time and got back in five or six weeks. Rutherford came to me with a very serious look on his face, and said, "Brother, you were so sure that a few weeks after the *Tower* would get out with that special notice in it that there would be enough funds come in here to build the factory. Here it's been six or eight weeks and just a few little dribbles have come in."

"Brother Rutherford, you haven't been out amongst our people as I have. The friends have their money in savings banks or hidden away in a glass jar under the cellar stairs or in the rafters of the barn—who knows where it is? Give them a little time. They'll think it over—it will be two or three months before it will begin to come in. Now I'm going away on another trip and I'll be back in about two months, and if there's not enough in here then to build that factory, I'll take you out and get you the finest chicken dinner we can get in Brooklyn." (He always did like chicken.) "And if there is enough in there, then Brother Martin and I will be looking for that chicken as your treat."

I left on my next speaking trip then and came back in eight weeks. I met Rutherford in the hallway and I said, "Well, Brother Rutherford, how are the subscriptions for loans coming in?"

"Oversubscribed—had to send some back."

"Well," I said, "I have a thousand dollars in my pocket that's been offered."

"Send it back, we don't need it." And we certainly didn't; we had more than enough.

Instead of borrowing money from a bank, we had borrowed it from our own people and the Society gave them a note at the regular rate of interest, although many of Jehovah's witnesses waived the interest. It was understood by those receiving notes that they could request their money in full at any time if they might unexpectedly have need for it. These received their money at once and the rest were paid off as the regular voluntary contributions made it possible. Before the notes had matured, all had been settled.

This arrangement certainly reminded me of the account in the Bible when Moses was told to build the Tabernacle for Jehovah in the wilderness.[3] Moses called the nation of Israel together and itemized the materials that would be needed and asked those of willing heart to contribute what they had. After awhile the men assigned to do the work told Moses: "The people bring much more than enough for the service of the work, which the Lord commanded to make. . . . So the people were restrained from bringing. For the stuff they had was sufficient for all the work to make it, and too much."

By 1946 we needed additions to the factory and in 1955 we needed an entire new building of thirteen floors. Both were built with money loaned the Society by Jehovah's witnesses themselves. In neither case were new notes given out until all previous ones were settled.

THE FAMILY FORMS A PATTERN

Such an arrangement would not be possible except for the fact that all of Jehovah's witnesses feel themselves a part of the organization. Actually, they are. The New World society is a family and Jehovah's spirit of giving poured out on them prompts them to support the work without their having to be asked.

Since 1901 my home has been in and out of Bethel. All this while I have enjoyed the close relationship that exists in our headquarters family. Our seventy-eight branch homes, too, while not nearly so large, operate on the same principles. So do our more than two hundred missionary homes. Like any family, we have our own rooms where we can withdraw for privacy, but we eat together and work together; our laundry is taken care of; our beds are made and our rooms are cleaned, all the work being done by those assigned to their particular tasks. The whole family is a happy lot and extremely considerate and thoughtful of one another.

Our meals are particularly sociable. At Bethel we have about fifty tables, each seating ten persons, and our entire family of 450 sits down together. The Society's president, N. H. Knorr, is head of the family and presides at our meals. He and his wife live at Bethel with the rest of us and so do all the directors of the Society. Like all the rest of us, in addition to board and room, they all get their $14 a month allowance for personal needs.

At breakfast we always have a short period of worship with a discussion of a Bible text for that day. This is always a stimulating period and gives us the right mental and spiritual start for the day's activity. After breakfast Knorr always remains in the dining room for a time so that any member of the family who has a question about his work or some personal problem can have it settled without need to make an appointment. For a man with the responsibility he has, Knorr is one of the most approachable men I have known. He has a deep personal interest in every member of the family.

Almost every family of Jehovah's witnesses I know who are all, or almost all, active in the Christian ministry follow about the same pattern of living. I've traveled around this country and Europe for many years, and practically all of the time I have been entertained in the homes of Jehovah's witnesses themselves. Everywhere I go I find the family arrangement is always the same amongst those who are really a part of the New World society; and at once I am made to feel a part of the family.

When they get up in the morning they always have the morning text read, then perhaps a brief discussion, with the father usually summing it up from printed comments for the day in the current *Yearbook of Jehovah's Witnesses*. The children are encouraged to participate and generally show real aptitude.

This sort of family relationship is something that the world has almost forgotten. Even modern churches don't have it. It's old-fashioned now for people to associate together as a Christian family. How many families do you know that read the Bible in the home and have family worship? or even return thanks at their meals? Yet this failure is considered by many sociologists and by many who are concerned with the problem of juvenile delinquency as one of the outstanding causes for broken homes and criminal youth.

IDENTIFYING THE FAMILY OF GOD

The family is the foundation of society, of the world. And just as the family is, so you might expect the whole nation to be. That is why, with the strong family unit built up in the homes of Jehovah's witnesses, the New World society is really a large family. When they come to their congregational meetings, or share in their house-to-house ministry, the individual family groups make up the larger family group, for they are all acting in the same way. They all live under the same principles at home. When they come to their "Kingdom Hall" for their meetings they come there to study, to be informed on the doctrines of the Bible and proper methods of preaching, to ask questions or to offer their comments. Then when they come together in a large convention it is just another family arrangement on a larger scale. Instead of having a few in a home, or 50 or 150 in a Kingdom Hall, they have 50,000 or 100,000 in a great stadium. It is the same family, all "brothers" and "sisters" in the New World society, bound together in relationship through Jesus Christ and the true worship of the Most High God, with prospects of some day filling the earth with their way of life.

That's why our movement is truly international. It bridges all national barriers, for it is the same world-wide. We live according to one standard, a rule that unites us as one regardless of any other affiliation, for it has its origin in the one Book, the Bible, and operates under the one unifying active force, the holy spirit of God. Do you think that is possible? Consider what the Bible says about the family of God. Jesus showed the closeness of this relationship even beyond that of fleshly ties with his mother, Mary, and his natural brothers, for he said: [4] "Who is my mother? and who are my brethren? And he stretched forth his hand toward his disciples, and said, Behold my mother and my brethren! For whosoever shall do the will of my Father which is in heaven, the same is my brother, and sister, and mother."

What reason do we have for saying it should be different on earth today? This unity existed within the early congregation. Why not now? Do you find it in your church?

Wouldn't you like to feel yourself a part of the family of God? You can. As surely as I have. From out of this world of people who do not know where our civilization is heading, you can find the right religion that will answer your questions about God as mine have been answered and make life worth living. It may be a struggle but it is worth it, and you can find it if you follow the way God has outlined for us in his Word.

CHAPTER 16

YOU CAN LIVE FOREVER

I HAVE CONSIDERED with you the ups and downs of over half a century of my personal association and activity with Jehovah's witnesses. Now, I come to the conclusion of my story. But, although it may bring my story to a close, it is by no means the end.

I am an old man in my eightieth year, yet life is just beginning—for me and for millions of those now living who may never die. Would you like to be one of these?

When I became associated with this group of zealous Christians, those who were active in the ministry could be numbered in the hundreds. Today they are numbered in hundreds of thousands. The prophecy,[1] "A little one shall become a thousand, and a small one a strong nation:" has begun fulfillment in my lifetime and I have seen it taking place.

This is just one of the prophecies I've seen fulfilled. I've told you of many and how they've strengthened my faith. From my youth I wanted to know what the future held for this world and for its inhabitants who live here such fleeting years.

To know its destiny is a comfort, but to know that our destiny is tied up with it is a blessing from God. Early in life I learned these things and have carried them with me constantly as an assurance of the future. I have shared this hope with thousands and am happy I have been able to share it with you.

JEHOVAH DETERMINES THE WAY OF LIFE

In telling you of my religion I've tried to show you why I'm convinced it's the right religion; why I'm convinced that religion is not a philosophy just to control man's behavior, or a formal ritual to prepare the "soul" for a "hereafter." I've tried to show you that the right religion is a way of life, a changed pattern of thinking in order to conform to specific requirements God has established for all who will have his approval. I've tried to picture to you a completely new world society that is living that religion, that is rising out of the present order of greedy, wicked and selfish systems; a society that is composed of people from all races, kindreds and tongues, yet united in the common worship of God.

I have pointed out why this new way of life became necessary; how our first parents, Adam and Eve, disobeyed God's righteous requirements and brought on us a condemnation of death; how the influence of Satan over the earth for nearly six thousand years has made it a place of sorrow, suffering and dread; how death has stalked through the earth with no one to stop its ravages. I have reminded you how Christ Jesus redeemed mankind by giving his life a ransom nearly two thousand years ago, yet the enemy death still reigns supreme over humanity and, while men have vainly tried to improve their conditions, little progress has been made because Satan is still at large and is the god of this system of things.[2]

Because of these conditions, only Jehovah God is in a position to correct the situation. His purpose to do so and how he will accomplish it form the theme of the entire Bible, as I have explained in my story. Whether we will benefit by God's program of activity depends entirely on how we view it and whether we are willing to accept it and gladly fulfill his requirements for us.

Don't think you can get into God's new world by taking "the way of your own choice." *We* don't make the requirements that must be met. God does. That is only reasonable. No country of this world permits prospective nationals to stipulate individually the terms by which they should be recognized and accepted. Why should God? Every government has its own regulations and you must comply with them strictly, or you'll never be accepted as a national of that government. So don't believe false representatives of God's government who say, "You can get into God's kingdom through the church of your choice. Pick out the one you like best and go to it. Just be good and be sincere. God will take care of you." He won't. Not that way.

Jesus said in the conclusion of his Sermon on the Mount: [3] "Enter by the narrow gate; for the gate is wide and the way is easy, that leads to destruction, and those who enter by it are many. For the gate is narrow and the way is hard, that leads to life, and those who find it are few." Then Jesus warned us against those not bringing forth the good fruit of his kingdom and said they would be destroyed. But those that built their house of faith on the rock-foundation would be saved.

WHY MY FAITH HAS SURVIVED

What is the rock foundation? And how do we build on it? Early in his study of the Bible, C. T. Russell recognized that our way of approach to Jehovah is through the only one that

God has appointed, Jesus Christ. Since Jesus gave his life a ransom for us he has purchased us; and therefore if we are to come to God we must come through him, listening to his wise words and heeding them. No one else, living or dead, can serve as a mediator. This provision, then, is the foundation on which our faith is built. Russell recognized this and realized it was now God's time to make its benefits available to mankind; therefore, he spent his lifetime building on that foundation by preaching the good news all over the world.

I've told you about the Society that grew up through this preaching, just as the prophecies had foretold; how I became a part of the movement, dedicating myself to God's service and being baptized in symbol of it; and how all of us who were added to this congregation recognized the obligation on us to preach also. But since Satan is the god of the present wicked system of things that operates men's affairs and controls their thinking from birth, and since he is still at large and bent on preventing any of the human race from getting out from under his control, he has hated the preaching work with extreme bitterness and has poured out his venom on Jehovah's persistent preachers through any means or agency he could dominate. I've given you concrete instances, perhaps much to your surprise that the leading religions of Christendom were the chief ones who played into his hands and permitted themselves to be his tools in an effort to suppress or destroy the message of God's blessing and judgment. The evidences are overwhelming that this is so. The methods themselves that these systems have used brand them as being of their father the Devil, for they duplicate in modern times the works performed against Jesus by those Satan used then.[4]

I have related to you how this new system of things has been violently opposed from its inception; how it was hunted down and buried in death during the closing years of World War I, only to survive and come to a startling rebirth in a new way of life as a new nation, a New World society.

I explained how this violent, unrelenting opposition almost drove the work underground on a global scale during World War II, but how the divinely-appointed theocratic arrangement enabled it to continue and even to expand numerically. No instrument devised against it has been able to stamp it out.[5] Neither will any power in heaven and earth be able to prevent its continued growth.[6] That is because it is ordained of God. It is in fulfillment of his own Word. Its life force is his holy spirit.

Can you wonder why my faith is strong? It has had to be to survive these extreme pressures brought against it. And can you wonder why my confidence in the New World society is unshaken, why I am convinced it is the planting and building of God, not man? I have seen men try to wreck it from inside the organization, just as deliberately as those who fought it from without. But I've seen these men discredited by their own actions and finally separated by their own choice; yet the theocratic society has remained intact in structure as well as in its standards of conduct. I've seen all vestiges of creature worship, the plague of Christendom, rooted out and the name of Jehovah given its rightful place of due honor.

THE ONLY PRACTICAL WAY IS GOD'S

Through this Society I've found a companionship and brotherhood with men of all nations and races. It has convinced me that men who have been total strangers all their lives can have complete confidence in each other and can become fast friends in a few hours' time. This is because we already have the firm foundation of a common understanding of our Creator and of his will for us and are strictly bound by the same high moral standards, regardless of how those peoples from whom we are extracted may live. We know that to violate these principles for a momentary advantage may cost us our everlasting life.

To us, it is not worth that. So, we can safely trust one another, and do.

I would not want you to conclude from this that Jehovah's witnesses are gullible or easily "taken in" by imposters. A faker in our midst is as easy to identify as a leopard amongst sheep. You can't counterfeit or sham the principles that Jehovah's witnesses live by or put them on and take them off like a coat. If they do not become a part of you by a continued cultivating of God's spirit, Jehovah will weed you out and separate you from his organization. I have seen it happen.

Hundreds of thousands of persons are recognizing that the wicked system of things that is Satan's world cannot continue its downward trend much longer and continue to exist. They observe the course of action being taken by Jehovah's witnesses and the standards by which their New World society is conducted, and they are in full sympathy with it. Their own hearts, feeling after righteousness, go out to a people who are making a sincere effort to stay clear of the vice and corruption of the world and who are endeavoring to honor and praise the name of the Most High God. They eagerly grasp and devour all the knowledge that is available about the new world promised in sacred prophecy and seek to obtain positive proofs that it is reasonable, that it is a tangible reality. Investigation provides such proofs in abundance.

It is already apparent to thinking persons that we have approached a turning-point in history. Oh, it's true, you'll hear some social reformers claiming that the viewpoint of Jehovah's witnesses is foolish, in looking to God to accomplish the permanent cure for the world's ills. Yet while these critics continue to struggle along by man's means, Jehovah's witnesses are already living, as a society, the reforms the world seeks. No matter how our enemies may vilify our society, condemn our ideals or criticize our practices—the record speaks for itself. Jehovah's witnesses do live together in peace. We do not go onto the "field of battle" and shoot each other because we happen to be born in different parts of the earth.[7] Neither are we divided within ourselves by conflicting doctrines, opinions and party factions.[8] These differences have been resolved quite simply. We are theocratically united in our common worship of God.

If so-called "practical" opposers could point to the same or better results within their own organizations, then perhaps their arguments in behalf of their own systems would be believable. They're like the man who saw a giraffe in the zoo for the first time. He stared at it in amazement for a moment and then said, "There ain't such an animal."

But the New World society *is* real. It may look strange to the man without faith, but results of its activity can be seen in the changing pattern of the lives of a growing multitude of persons. It's just that opposers refuse to recognize and acknowledge the power of God and his spirit upon his people.

THERE IS NO MIDDLE GROUND

You, and every other living person in the world today, are facing the most significant crisis mankind will ever encounter. We have reached a time of judgment. It is not just the survival of modern governments that is at issue. The entire concept of rule by man is in the balance.

The issue is sharp and clear: Will you continue to support and bear up this present system of things that is filling the earth with suffering, sorrow, sin and death? Or will you choose and fit yourself for God's love-filled new world?

You must decide. You will take one way or the other. There is no middle course.

If you decide in favor of this doomed world you must reconcile yourself to meeting its fate. But if you choose to cast your lot with those who are upholding the standard of

God's righteousness, you have a prospect of endless life in peace and happiness with real freedom.

The line of demarcation between the two sides is definite. It is a rapidly widening chasm. Soon that division will be so complete there will be no more passing over from one side to the other. When that time arrives the preaching of the good news will have accomplished its purpose. Then the last lost and strayed sheep will have been found and brought into the "one flock" of the One Shepherd. Then the spiritual prosperity of the New World society will have reached a new peak. The time will have come for the "time of the end" to close, for the days of tribulation upon Satan's world to be shortened no longer for the sake of God's chosen ones. The time will have come for the wicked system of things under Satan to meet its accomplished end. Then the final war will begin. That war is the battle of the great day of God, the Almighty. It is called in scripture, Armageddon.[9] None will survive except those who have taken God's side of the issue we now face.

HOW YOU MAY TAKE GOD'S SIDE

What must you do to take God's side? What course must you follow now to find God's favor and protection during Armageddon? The first step must be to recognize the need. If you don't believe the world of mankind is estranged from God and must seek his favor, if you're not convinced that this world is approaching its complete end, then you may not see the need to do anything at all. So the obvious answer to that is to investigate.

You must take the first step, exercising faith in God.[10] "Without faith it is impossible to please him. For whoever would draw near to God must believe that he exists and that he rewards those who seek him." If the time is really here for Jehovah God to settle accounts and take over the kingdom rulership of earth, nothing could be of greater importance to you, and anyone who would attempt to dissuade you from learning of it is not your friend. To consider the evidences that Jehovah's witnesses present to you as testimony costs you nothing but your time. If, after careful study of the facts, you are not convinced, you have lost nothing. On the other hand, you may recognize that you have not yet begun to live. Jehovah's witnesses earnestly repeat the words of warning Moses spoke to the Israelites as they prepared to enter the Promised Land: [11] "I call heaven and earth to witness against you this day, that I have set before you life and death, blessing and curse; therefore choose life, that you and your descendants may live."

You must repent of your past course [12] and be converted or turned around from following the way of this world and base your actions on the standards of God's Word.[13] That means you must recognize your only approach to God is through Jesus and the merit of his shed blood as your ransom.[14] Thus you accept God's way of doing things and follow the example of Jesus and others in unconditionally dedicating yourself to God to do his will.[15] As a symbol of dedication, to show that your will is now alive to God's and you're seeking to conform your thinking to his requirements, you must be baptized by total immersion in water.[16]

Study of God's Word will acquaint you with his purpose and what he expects from you as his servant. Paul said: [17] "Necessity is laid upon me. Woe to me if I do not preach the gospel!" If you become convinced this necessity is laid upon you, then you must be properly trained for the ministry, not by attending expensive schools for years of unprofitable study of philosophy, sociology and similar subjects. You are now interested in getting the mind of God, so you study God's Word, the Bible, and enlarge your ability by putting into practical use what you learn. Thus you help others as you are

being helped. Paul admonished a very young minister: [18]
"Take heed to yourself and to your teaching; hold to that,
for by so doing you will save both yourself and your hearers."
That is the way the entire New World society is being pre-
pared to inhabit the system of things that will operate when
Armageddon is over.

RESTORATION OF EDENIC CONDITIONS

After the raging fury of Armageddon has spent itself in the
destruction of the enemies of Jehovah and righteousness, a
serene calm will settle over the earth, as on the sea of Galilee
after Jesus rebuked the storm. All human beings brought
through the battle will be fully dedicated to Jehovah and will
then carry on the new work assigned to them, just as they are
now being trained to serve God.

Everyone you meet will have a kind word for you and will
seek to do you good. Earth will be a grand place to live. The
old selfish system of greed and graft will not be there but
the law of brotherly love will prevail where each one will
love his neighbor as himself. With love at work, gone are
jealousies and disputes, and in their stead we see patient kindness as men and women carry out the commands of their
gracious God Jehovah.

Confronted as we are with sickness, suffering and death,
we may find it difficult to imagine that life could be different.
But beyond Armageddon, in our generation, human beings
shall live forever in God's new world. Look at these men and
women as the restoration work progresses. Radiant with health
and beauty, they are perfect in form and feature, for the
prophecy foretells that a man can return to the days of his
youth and his flesh can become like a child's in freshness.[19]
What an experience it will be to reverse life's journey and
grow younger each year instead of older! Mental, moral and

physical perfection will stamp the features of all who complete the journey. As for wars, they shall cease,[20] and death will be no more.[21] "Behold, the dwelling of God is with men. He will dwell with them, and they shall be his people, and God himself will be with them; he will wipe away every tear from their eyes, and death shall be no more, neither shall there be mourning nor crying nor pain any more, for the former things have passed away."

After mankind has reached a measure of perfection, they will be told to make preparations for the restoration of their beloved dead. What a happy thing it will be to prepare a room for Mother and Dad! Some day while working about your lovely garden park home you will hear the familiar voice of father or mother calling from the room you prepared for them. You will run to their room and tell them about the new world and its joys and all the things that happened on earth while they were asleep in death. How happy they will be to have no more pain, for they will come back without the sickness that caused their death, and they will have before them the glorious hope of living forever on the perfected earth! This process will go on until all in the memorial tombs are brought forth.[22] Thus we behold the original purpose of Jehovah, as stated in the second chapter of Genesis, fulfilled; to have this earth subdued and brought to the perfection exhibited in the garden of Eden, prepared as an example; to have it filled with perfect human creatures, accomplished to God's glory.

HOW MUCH DO YOU LOVE GOD?

Too good to be true, you say? On the contrary, would it not be poor reasoning to conclude that fallen man could think of a better arrangement for the future of creatures, made in the image of Jehovah, than the all-wise loving Creator, who says he loves his creatures more than a mother does her nursing child? Eternity in perfection and boundless happiness is his promise. His purposes cannot and will not fail.

After every war there is a necessary period of rehabilitation. That means that those who will represent the King, Jesus Christ, must be trained and equipped before the final war so that no period of anarchy will immediately follow it. The New World society is being prepared now by the many lessons it has learned and by its experiences in operating under all kinds of conditions, favorable and unfavorable. As a result, there is being developed world-wide, a society of hundreds of thousands of persons with a keen appreciation of God's righteous requirements who are willing to accept any cost to themselves rather than compromise or slacken their hold on the way of life that is pleasing to God. They do this because they love God more than anything else. Talk to them when they come to your door. They will be pleased to help you as they themselves have been helped.

Have you ever asked yourself: "How much do I really love God? If I were to find that God's Word, the Bible, contradicted what I have always believed, which would I follow? If I had to choose between some respected or dearly-loved individual and my Creator, what would be my decision? If I were suddenly forbidden by law to worship God, if continued worship might cost me my life, what would I do?"

You may some day be confronted with such circumstances to determine whether you have the right religion. It may be a real battle for you, but I am sure that if you make the right choice it will give you peace of mind and will be pleasing to God. I have been faced with each one of these decisions and many others also, and today I am more determined than ever to keep on in my faith. It has made life worth living for me. It is still helping me to face the future without fear.

I hope my story will help you to do the same. If it does, then it will have been worth the telling.

REFERENCES *

Chapter 1

1. *Millennial Dawn*, Vol. 1 (1886) pp. 187–188.
2. Job 14:13–15; 3:17–19, *American Standard Version.*

Chapter 2

1. Romans 12:2, *New World Translation.*
2. Proverbs 3:5, 6.
3. Acts 17:11.
4. Ecclesiastes 9:5, 10; Romans 6:23.
5. Genesis 1:27, 28; 2:16, 17.
6. Genesis 3:17–19.
7. Genesis 4:1.
8. Romans 5:12.
9. 1 Corinthians 15:17, 18.
10. Luke 19:10.
11. Hebrews 2:14, 15.
12. 2 John 7.
13. Exodus 21:23, 24.
14. Matthew 20:28.

---

* Note: All Biblical references are to the Authorized (King James) Version, except where specifically stated otherwise.

15. 1 Peter 3:18; 1 Timothy 6:16.

16. Luke 24:32.

17. Matthew 13:24–30.

18. The full significance of the Greek word *parousia* here used is clearly demonstrated in relation to its antithesis, *apousia*, at Philippians 2:12: "Ye have always obeyed, not as in my presence [*parousia*] only, but now much more in my absence [*apousia*]."

19. *Herald of the Morning*, Vol. 7, No. 1, July, 1878, p. 11.

20. *Zion's Watch Tower*, Vol. 15, No. 8 ("Extra Edition"), April 25, 1894, pp. 101–104.

21. John 11:11–14, 23, 24.

22. Hebrews 12:13.

23. 2 Corinthians 11:3, 14.

24. Philippians 2:5–8.

Chapter 3

1. 1 Corinthians 3:6, *New World Translation*.

2. Genesis 12:1–3.

3. Galatians 3:8, 16, 27, 29.

4. Jeremiah 20:9.

5. *Millennial Dawn*, Vol. 1 (1886 edition), p. 174.

6. *See:* Hebrews 2:16; Philippians 2:7, 8; John 1:14.

7. Philippians 2:7.

Chapter 4

1. *The Watch Tower*, Vol. 35, No. 1, January 1, 1914, pp. 4, 5.

2. Luke 21:24.

3. 1 Chronicles 29:23, *American Standard Version*.

4. 2 Kings 25:1–12.

5. This date is determined as follows: The length of Jerusalem's desolation was foretold as 70 years. (2 Chronicles 36:21) It was also foretold her captor, Babylon, would be destroyed at the end of that time. (Jeremiah 25:11, 12; compare Daniel 9:2) The most authoritative archaeological evidence shows Babylon as overthrown October 7, 539 B.C. (See: *Babylonian Chronology 626 B.C.-A.D. 45*, by Richard Anthony Parker and Waldo Herman Dubberstein [Chicago, 1942: The University of Chicago Press], p. 11.) This would be the *accession* year of Cyrus, successor Persian king. The following April, 538 B.C., would begin his first *regnal* year. (See: *The Mysterious Numbers of the Hebrew Kings*, by Edwin Richard Thiele [Chicago, 1951: The University of Chicago Press], p. 14.) Within that year a decree was issued for the release of the Jews and by the fall they

had begun to resettle Jerusalem. (Ezra 1:1; 3:1, 2) Therefore, since the foretold 70-year desolation ended in the fall of 537 B.C., it must have begun in the fall of 607 B.C. with Jerusalem's destruction. [NOTE: Although the archaeological evidences referred to here were not known in 1914, they have since only served to refine and corroborate Russell's calculations. For a detailed discussion see *The Watchtower*, Vol. 73, No. 9, May 1, 1952, pp. 265 ff.]

6. Ezekiel 21:25–27.
7. Psalm 110:1, 2; Daniel 2:44.
8. Luke 21:24, 27.
9. Matthew 2:3–6; Luke 3:15; 7:19, 20; John 1:19–21.
10. Daniel 4:32.
11. Numbers 14:34; Ezekiel 4:6.
12. *The Watch Tower*, Vol. 35, No. 9, May 1, 1914, p. 135.
13. Matthew 24:34.
14. Proverbs 13:12, *Revised Standard Version*.
15. New York *World*, August 30, 1914, Sunday magazine, pp. 4, 17.
16. *The Watch Tower*, Vol. 36, No. 4, February 15, 1915, p. 53.
17. Washington (D. C.) *Times Herald*, March 13, 1945, editorial.
18. Dr. Harold C. Urey, in Cleveland *Plain Dealer*, December 9, 1951.
19. Prof. Rene Albrecht-Carrié, in *Scientific Monthly* (Washington, D. C., American Association for the Advancement of Science), Vol. 73, No. 1, July, 1951, p. 16.
20. Edmonton (Alberta, Canada) *Journal*, August 7, 1954, editorial.
21. New York *Times Magazine*, August 1, 1954.
22. Pittsburgh *Sun-Telegraph*, August 1, 1954, editorial.
23. *Zion's Watch Tower*, Vol. 1, No. 3, September, 1879, pp. 1, 2.
24. Revelation 12:7–10.
25. Daniel 12:1; 2:44; Isaiah 9:6, 7.
26. Matthew 24:22.
27. Revelation 16:14–16.
28. Revelation 7:9, 10.
29. Acts 1:6.

Chapter 5

1. Matthew 20:1–16.
2. 1 Peter 4:17; Matthew 24:10, 12.
3. 1 Peter 4:12, *Revised Standard Version*.
4. John 13:35, *Revised Standard Version*.
5. Luke 12:37.
6. Matthew 24:45–51.
7. Malachi 3:1–3, *American Standard Version*.

Chapter 6

1. Revelation 11:3.

2. Title of a series of tracts published by the International Bible Students Association.

3. Bell (1856–1919), an exceptionally brilliant military leader, had been Chief of Staff of the United States Army (1906–1910). He suffered a fatal heart attack January 8, 1919. See *Encyclopedia Americana*, 1942 ed.

4. *Consolation* magazine, August 23, 1939, p. 5.

5. *Congressional Record* (Vol. 56, Part 6), Senate, April 24, 1918, p. 5542. Also New York *Times*, April 25, 1918, p. 12.

6. *Congressional Record* (Vol. 56, Part 6), Senate, May 4, 1918, p. 6051.

7. *Congressional Record* (Vol. 56, Part 6), Senate, May 4, 1918, p. 6052.

8. *Kingdom News*, Vol. 1, Nos. 1, 2 and 3, published by I. B. S. A. (International Bible Students Association), Brooklyn, N. Y., March 15, April 15 and May 1918, respectively. Publication resumed July, 1939 (Vol. 1, No. 4), by Watchtower Bible and Tract Society, Inc., and continued until February, 1946 (Vol. 1, No. 15).

9. *International Bible Students Association* was the generic term used from 1910 until 1931 to identify those unitedly sharing in Bible educational activities supervised by the Watch Tower Bible and Tract Society throughout the world. That term as so used until 1931 corresponds, since 1931, with use of the term *Jehovah's witnesses* to identify participants in the continuing earth-wide work, announcing Jehovah's kingdom. (See: *The Watch Tower*, Vol. 31, No. 7, April 1, 1910, pp. 119, 120; Vol. 34, No. 1, January 1, 1913, pp. 6, 7, "The Harvest Work World-wide"; Vol. 52, No. 19, October 1, 1931, pp. 291–297.) Incidentally, the mentioned generic use of the term "International Bible Students Association" from 1910 to 1931 should not be confused with use of the very same name chosen for the corporation created and registered at London, England, in 1914, and later also chosen for the Canadian corporation, for supervising the Watch Tower Society's activities in the United Kingdom and in Canada, respectively.

Chapter 7

1. Quotations are exactly as they appear in the court record.

2. *Ex parte Hudgings*, 249 U. S. 378 (April 14, 1919).

3. *Civil Liberty in War Time* by John Lord O'Brian (presented before the New York State Bar Association, January 17 and 18, 1919).

Harlan Fiske Stone by Alpheus Thomas Mason (New York, 1956: The Viking Press), p. 525.

4. See New York *Herald*, June 22, 1918, Part 2, p. 5.

5. Acts 6:9–15.

Chapter 8

1. This is the same Manton who, on December 4, 1939, was finally adjudged guilty of accepting bribes totaling $186,000 while serving as United States Circuit Judge. See *United States* v. *Manton*, 107 Federal (2d), p. 834.

2. 258 Federal, p. 855 (May 14, 1919).

3. *The Watch Tower*, Vol. 40, No. 18, September 15, 1919, pp. 279–281.

4. *The Watch Tower*, Vol. 40, No. 19, October 1, 1919, p. 296.

5. Matthew 24:14.

6. *The Watch Tower*, Vol. 41, No. 13, July 1, 1920, pp. 199, 200.

7. *The Watch Tower*, Vol. 43, No. 21, November 1, 1922, pp. 332 ff.

8. 1 Peter 2:5.

9. Malachi 3:1.

10. Isaiah 6:1–11.

11. Revelation 11:11.

Chapter 9

1. Ezekiel 9:2–4.

2. Mark 14:27.

3. Zechariah 13:7.

4. *Zion's Watch Tower*, Vol. 6, No. 2, October, 1884, p. 2, "Legal Incorporation."

5. *Zion's Watch Tower*, Vol. 25, No. 8, April 15, 1904, p. 125.

6. *The Watch Tower*, Vol. 44, No. 5, March 1, 1923, pp. 68, 69.

7. *The Watch Tower*, Vol. 52, No. 17, September 1, 1931, pp. 259 ff.

8. Luke 12:37; 2 Timothy 4:8.

9. Hebrews 1:1, 2.

10. Matthew 13:41.

11. 1 Corinthians 10:11, *New World Translation*.

12. Deuteronomy 7:7, *New World Translation*.

13. Psalm 106:8.

14. 1 Corinthians 1:11–13; 3:3, 11.

15. Galatians 5:9–12; 1:6–8, *New World Translation*.

16. 2 Timothy 2:16–18, *New World Translation*.

17. 2 Thessalonians 2:3, 7, *New World Translation*.

18. Acts 20:29-31, *New World Translation*.
19. 2 John 7, *New World Translation*.
20. 1 Peter 2:9, *New World Translation*.
21. 1 Thessalonians 5:21; 1 John 4:1; Acts 17:11; 2 Timothy 2:15.
22. Acts 17:6, 7.
23. Luke 23:14, 23, 24.
24. 2 Corinthians 13:5.
25. John 14:6.
26. Matthew 7:21.

Chapter 10

1. Luke 12:37, *Revised Standard Version*.
2. 2 Timothy 3:16, 17, *Douay*.
3. Exodus, Leviticus, Numbers, Deuteronomy, 2 Kings, Psalms, Isaiah and Jeremiah.
4. John 13:16; 1 John 4:9.
5. John 14:28, *Douay*.
6. Matthew 19:5, *Douay*.
7. Isaiah 1:18, *American Standard Version*.
8. Acts 20:29, 30; 2 Timothy 4:3, 4; 2 Peter 3:16.
9. 2 Peter 1:20, *New World Translation*.
10. Hebrews 5:11-14.
11. Proverbs 4:18.
12. Matthew 24:45, *New World Translation*.
13. Luke 12:32.
14. Revelation 7:4, 9.
15. Genesis 40:8.
16. Daniel 12:8-10, *American Standard Version*.
17. Acts 15:1-29.
18. Galatians 2:11-14, *New World Translation*.
19. John 6:60, 66.

Chapter 11

1. Luke 14:2-6.
2. Luke 6:13.
3. 1 Corinthians 12:18; Mark 10:40.
4. Ephesians 4:11-13.
5. Acts 15:1-21.
6. Titus 1:5.
7. Acts 6:1-6.
8. Acts 8:25; 1 Corinthians 9:16.
9. 1 Timothy 5:19-22; Hebrews 13:17.
10. Acts 13:2-4.

11. Acts 3:20, 21.
12. Isaiah 60:17, 22.
13. *The Watch Tower*, Vol. 59, Nos. 11, 12, June 1 and June 15, 1938, "Organization," Part 1 and Part 2.
14. 1 Timothy 3:10.

Chapter 12

1. Psalm 94:20, 21.
2. Matthew 5:7, *New World Translation*.
3. Matthew 23:33, *New World Translation*.
4. Jeremiah 1:10.
5. 2 Corinthians 10:3–5; Ephesians 6:17.
6. Don Rockwell (Ed.), *Radio Personalities*, 1936, p. 82.
7. Mark 12:17.
8. *Minersville* v. *Gobitis*, 310 U. S. 586 (June 3, 1940), 60 S. Ct. 1010, 87 L. Ed. 1375; reversed June 14, 1943, see chapter 13, note 2.
9. 2 Corinthians 5:20.
10. 1 John 5:21.
11. Acts 5:29.
12. Exodus 20:2–6.
13. Daniel 3.
14. 1 Corinthians 10:11, 14.
15. See: Victor W. Rotnem, "Recent Restrictions Upon Religious Liberty," *American Political Science Review* (Madison, Wis., The American Political Science Association), Vol. 36, No. 6, December, 1942, pp. 1053–1068.

Chapter 13

1. Revelation 12:16.
2. *West Virginia State Board of Education* v. *Barnette*, 319 U. S. 624 (June 14, 1943, "Flag day"), 63 S. Ct. 1178, 87 L. Ed. 1628, reversing *Minersville* v. *Gobitis*, 310 U. S. 586 (June 3, 1940); see chapter 12, note 8.
3. *Falbo* v. *United States*, 320 U. S. 549, January 3, 1944.
4. *Estep* v. *United States*, 327 U. S. 114, February 4, 1946.
5. Genesis 9:3–5; Leviticus 17:14; Acts 15:28, 29; 1 Chronicles 11:17–19.
6. Acts 28:3–5.
7. Jeremiah 26:14 [paraphrased].
8. Hebrews 12:3, 4, *Revised Standard Version*.
9. John 16:33, *Revised Standard Version*.

Chapter 14

1. 1 Peter 3:15.
2. *Our Sunday Visitor* (Our Sunday Visitor, Inc., Huntington, Ind.), Vol. 45, No. 3, May 20, 1956.
3. Zechariah 8:23.
4. John 8:32.
5. Deuteronomy 31:11–13.
6. Deuteronomy 6:6, 7.
7. Matthew 19:14.
8. Acts 4:13.
9. *Our Sunday Visitor* (Our Sunday Visitor, Inc., Huntington, Ind.), Vol. 45, Nos. 1, 2 and 3, May 6, 13 and 20, 1956, respectively.
10. *Our Sunday Visitor* (Our Sunday Visitor, Inc., Huntington, Ind.), Vol. 45, No. 5, June 3, 1956.
11. John 7:20; Matthew 11:19.
12. John 15:18–20.
13. John 21:15–17.
14. Acts 20:20.
15. Matthew 28:19, 20.

Chapter 15

1. Matthew 10:8.
2. Matthew 10:10.
3. Exodus 36:5–7.
4. Matthew 12:48–50. *See also* Matthew 10:37; 19:29.

Chapter 16

1. Isaiah 60:22.
2. 2 Corinthians 4:4.
3. Matthew 7:13–29, *Revised Standard Version.*
4. John 8:44.
5. Isaiah 54:17.
6. Isaiah 9:7.
7. Acts 17:26.
8. 1 Corinthians 1:10.
9. Revelation 16:14–16.
10. Hebrews 11:6, *Revised Standard Version.*
11. Deuteronomy 30:19, *Revised Standard Version.*
12. Matthew 4:17.
13. Romans 12:2.

14. John 14:6; Romans 3:23–25.
15. Hebrews 10:5–7; 11:24, 25.
16. Matthew 28:19, 20.
17. 1 Corinthians 9:16, *Revised Standard Version.*
18. 1 Timothy 4:16, *Revised Standard Version.*
19. Job 33:25.
20. Isaiah 2:4.
21. Revelation 21:3, 4, *Revised Standard Version.*
22. John 5:28, 29.

INDEX

237